Encounters with Angels

Odile Haumonté

Encounters with Angels
The Invisible Companions
of Our Spiritual Life

Translated by James Henri McMurtrie

SOPHIA INSTITUTE PRESS
Manchester, New Hampshire

Sophia Institute Press
Box 5284, Manchester, NH 03108
1-800-888-9344

www.SophiaInstitute.com

Sophia Institute Press® is a registered trademark of Sophia Institute.

paperback ISBN 978-1-64413-471-9

ebook ISBN 978-1-64413-472-6

Library of Congress Control Number: 2021940689

Third printing

Do not neglect to show hospitality to strangers,
for thereby some have entertained angels unawares.

—Hebrews 13:2

Contents

Part 3
Angels, Our Fellow Travelers

Encounters with Angels

Introduction

"An angel goes by": we use this expression when there is a sudden silence in the middle of a conversation. But do angels really pass through our lives? The Christian faith invites us to think that they do. God has given His angels, spiritual creatures who contemplate Him in His glory, the task of watching over us and accompanying us on the path of life.

I am especially grateful for angels, for, without them, I would perhaps not be here today. My mother told me that one day, while she was getting ready to cross the street, she had not seen a bus that was going the wrong way. When she started to step onto the road, she clearly felt a hand pull her backward. Nobody was there when she turned around. Thus, she advised me to pray to my guardian angel at all times. Without him, I would not have been born, and my priest brother would not have been either. I would not have had my five children. The world would not be the same without guardian angels.

An angel goes by and saves me.

An angel goes by and comforts me.

An angel goes by and guides me.

When an angel enters our life, it changes its course. We will see this in the lives of many saints and biblical figures, but this very vast subject will not be exhausted. We will approach the boundaries of theology, ecclesiology, exegesis, patristics, and hagiography to discover the traces that angels have left in human history. If, by chance, the edge of a wing strokes your face, let it be done. The angel's time is also the time of love.

So, are angels too far from us? Too strange? Too elusive?

Or are they devoted? Sincere? Faithful? Attentive?

The answer can be found throughout this book. We will see how angels intervene in the lives of the saints and in our own lives.

The appendix offers theological writings on the mystery of the existence of angels.

1

The Zero-Hour Encounter

I invite you to read this chapter while listening to
Gounod's *Ave Maria*, performed by Sarah Brightman.

He is not the first angel to reveal himself to men.

She is not the first young woman whom the Bible mentions
because of her deeds or her faith. There was Miriam, whose joy
radiated in inspired canticles. There were Judith and Esther,
those heroines who saved their endangered people.

Without this meeting between Gabriel and Mary, however,
the world's face would be very different, and we would undoubtedly not be here today.

Some authors assert that Mary was used to seeing angels. I do
not know. With God's permission, everything is possible. Many
saints have seen angels. But the saints also performed numerous
miracles, and Mary could probably have accomplished some during her life. Yet she did not do it. What she did that was more
exceptional was to keep in her heart all the events that occurred
in her life and to ponder them.

This humble young Galilean woman was in her parents' house
in Nazareth. What time was it? Was it dawn, whose gentle clarity
seems to promise us a purer and more beautiful world? Was it the

blaze of dusk, which invites our minds and hearts to relax after the weight of the day? Was it noon, the relentless time when anything might happen?

She was alone. Her hands were busy, and her heart was praying. She was probably humming, having been born into a people who, since the dawn of time, had sung its pain, anger, joy, and hope. She was not thinking of what she would do later or what she did this morning. She was completely in the present moment. She offered herself in that here and now, the only place and moment that belonged to her to such an extent that she could present them to the Lord in thanksgiving.

Suddenly, a light illuminated the room. This young girl with pure eyes knew how to perceive the light in the eyes of her contemporaries. But the light that made her turn around then did not look like anything she had ever seen. She may have been familiar with the angels and was certainly acquainted with the Bible. Therefore, Mary immediately understood the exceptional character of this angelic manifestation.

Gabriel, whose name means "strength of God," softened the radiance of his splendor to enter the very simple dwelling. But his glow set the room ablaze, each object reflecting this light, which offered a glimpse of the first days of Creation. Mary was not frightened. What could she fear since she had put all her trust in God? Yet she was startled while facing such a majestic being! Did this heavenly messenger really leave the Lord's throne to come to her?

"Hail, Mary, full of grace, the Lord is with thee."

She was completely confused! The radiant angel's visit amazed her. But his words—or one of his words—overwhelmed her. How we would love to know more! How we would want to probe Mary's heart in order to pierce the mystery! What word was disturbing her to this extent? Was it the respect that she perceived in the "Hail" of this angel of light, who seemed to bow down before her — this little human creature who was still holding the little jug that she was wiping or the bread dough that she was kneading? Was it this unfathomable promise "the Lord is with thee," when she was the one who was in her Creator's presence day and night? Finally, was it this reception of grace that became a name in the archangel's mouth? In this instance, Mary may have understood the mystery of her Immaculate Conception. Having been preserved from Original Sin, she suddenly better comprehended what distinguished her from other women, from the young village girls, and even from her beloved mother. She had never sinned. So that is what this irreducible distance and space within her, which was like an enclosed garden, was all about. She was completely overwhelmed by it. Why such a favor? Above all, how did the work of salvation start in the world?

"Mary, be without fear."

Their dialogue, which led to the yes that would save the world, would develop respectfully and sincerely. But, for the moment, she remained silent. Mary: her name was given to her again. She was the Immaculate Conception. But, at the same time, she continued to be little Mary of Nazareth. God's grace did not sweep away her identity. It transcended and inhabited her.

Gabriel thought it was worth it. All that had been experienced was nothing before the beauty of this moment. This included the revolt of the angels, the history of men with their falls and recoveries, the holy kings and bad kings, the great prophets and false prophets, the exiles and returns, and even the rebellious Zechariah. (He was the cousin in Judea who was forced to be mute.) The marvelous choice of this pure young woman began to undo the knot of all of humanity's sins in one instant. Eve's disobedience, Adam's passivity, Cain's crime, and all the iniquities that followed melted like wax in the clear flame of this contemplative face. That, therefore, is what the Most High God contemplated when He looked into Eve's eyes for the answer to His question: "What have you done?"

When the angel left, humanity's salvation was underway. A little Child, who was starting to develop His body in the cradle of the maternal womb, responded to His Mother: "Here I am." The angels joyfully exulted in the heavens. How was it possible that nobody heard their songs of joy and glory?

The Courage to Say Yes

Though we are not always able to do it, we try to follow in Jesus' footsteps in order to advance on our path. We are not born preserved from sin; but when we receive absolution in the Sacrament of Reconciliation, we become pure like Mary for a time. We have not been chosen from all eternity to give the Savior to the world; but after we receive Communion, we really carry Jesus' living Body in our flesh for a time. We are, like Mary, tabernacles of His Real Presence, and we may say to her, "When the white host comes into my heart, Jesus, Your Sweet Lamb, thinks He is resting in you!"[1]

What is the "zero hour" in this chapter's title? Agatha Christie mentions it in a 1944 novel as being the pivotal point when all the elements are gathered together and all the puzzle pieces are put into place:

---

[1] St. Thérèse of the Child Jesus and the Holy Face, "Why I Love You, O Mary."

All converging towards a given spot. ... And then, when the time comes—over the top! Zero Hour. Yes, all of them converging towards zero.[2]

She explained her idea during a dialogue between a nurse and her patient:

"I've got a right to do what I like with my own life."

"No—no, you haven't. ... You don't understand. God may need you. ... It may be just by being somewhere—not doing anything—just by being at a certain place at a certain time."

Each of us has experienced or will experience our zero hour, which we can call our conversion or new birth. It is when our lives make sense, when everything becomes clear, and when we know why we came to this earth, into this place, into this family, and at this time.

The Strength and Freedom of the Will

We can evade our zero hour. Mary was free to say no to the angel. Gabriel was free not to carry the divine message to Mary. Jesus was free not to go up to Jerusalem, where death awaited Him.[3] Saul was free to get back up after his fall, shake the dust off his clothes, and continue on his path without ever becoming Paul. As Catherine of Siena wrote:

We still see man's strength and freedom in you today, O Mary. For it was after the deliberation of the majestic

---

[2] Agatha Christie, *Toward Zero* (1944), prologue.

[3] "They were looking for Jesus and saying to one another as they stood in the temple, 'What do you think? That he will not come to the feast?'" (John 11:56).

Trinity that an angel was sent to you to announce the mystery of divine guidance and ask for your consent. Before descending into your womb, the Son of God spoke to your freedom. He waited at the door of your will. He offered you the desire He had to live in you. He would never have come if you had not said to Him: "Here I am, the servant of the Lord; let it be with me according to your word" (Luke 1:38). Is that not real proof of the strength and freedom of the will? Nothing good or evil can be done without it. Neither the devil nor any creature forces it to sin, if it does not become their accomplice. And nobody can force it to do good if it wants to resist. Thus, man's will is free. O Mary, Almighty God knocked on your door. If you had not opened your will to Him, He would not have taken on human nature.[4]

Would it not be simple if, when we make poor choices and on all our highways and byways, we would find an angel with a sheathed sword who would order us to get back on the right path?[5] There is only one problem. God respects our freedom so much that He will never force us to be peaceful and happy and experience His love. He allows us to be free to choose the sad and dark path of cursing even though we can be so happy by blessing others and saying good things!

Hergé showed this in a funny way in the Tintin comics. We see Captain Haddock and Snowy being overcome by

[4] Prayer on the Annunciation (1379).
[5] See Num. 22:21–35 (Balaam and the donkey). See also Gen. 3:24: "At the east of the garden of Eden he placed the cherubim, and a flaming sword which turned every way, to guard the way to the tree of life."

temptation. Good angels who look like the characters draw them toward goodness while their devil twins try to lead them to drink or to disobey. The theologian Origen told us: "All men have two angels beside them. One of them is a bad one who drives them to sin. The other is a good one who urges them to choose the path of virtue."

In fact, we are offered much happiness when our freedom encounters God's will. When it does, we have found our niche and are adjusted—that it to say, on the way to becoming just and holy. It is a work that needs to be restarted every day. Mary also needed to do this. She had to say yes again when she left for Bethlehem toward the end of her pregnancy, when she went into exile in Egypt, when Joseph died, and when she stood at the foot of the Cross.

> Faced with the Gospel's call to say yes for one's whole life, the question sometimes arises: How will I persevere? We long to say yes, but it can be frightening, and there is hesitation. One day, however, we will be astonished to find ourselves already following Jesus. The yes had already been present in the depths of our being.[6]

I love those old Christian novels that nourished French women in the interwar years up to the 1950s. I have from my mother some books by Berthe Bernage and Elizabeth Goudge as well as the magazine *Suzette's Week*. They are yellowed and dog-eared from being heavily read. They speak of a society that has disappeared and the beautiful values that are cherished and transmitted from mothers to daughters. This can be seen in a dialogue between Brigitte, from Berthe Bernage's *Brigitte et les routes*

---

6   Brother Roger Schutz from Taizé.

Nouvelles, and her daughter. Brigitte worries over the prospect of a long professional trip that her husband envisions:

> "I did not accept what he wanted. Then, suddenly, I do not know what happened. I understood, and I accepted.... Mimi, I am sure that you were praying."
> She blushed.
> "But yes. We had to help you."
> "You are, all in all, our guardian angel."[7]

"Your Voice Is Gentle"

I was a very complicated child who turned things around in my head a hundred times. I easily and frequently said no, and I had a hard time saying yes without several mental convolutions. But God is simple. This beautiful word, *simple*, has been emptied of its meaning! I recall a discussion in which this quality was attributed to someone: "She was simple." I immediately retorted: "Not at all. She was intelligent and cultured." A debate had ensued that showed me that the words are not contradictory—quite the opposite. It is really sad that *simple* is taken to mean "stupid" or "simpleminded" today.

To be simple means to get straight to the point, to see the crux of the matter, and to get rid of whatever distracts us from our goal or weighs us down. Angels help us, like older brothers who are more perfect but compassionate in the face of our weaknesses. They are faithful companions who want to encourage us to live like them in the sight of God.

---

7   Berthe Bernage, *Brigitte et les routes Nouvelles* [Brigitte and the new roads] (Vanves: Éditions Gautier-Languereau, 1950), 35–36.

Are we attentive enough? When God's angel comes to talk to me, am I busy on my cell phone, immersed in a book, or glued to the television? When am I available to listen to the voice of the angel beside me? Do I welcome him when he wants to entrust me with a mission or clarify the meaning of my life for me? His voice is so gentle that noise covers it up. He is so respectful that he will not bother me or impose himself. He is so patient that he can await my response for several years.

✵ Today, Lord, I want to listen to You. I want to say yes to You:
- yes to the life You are giving me here and now
- yes to my family, those who are close to me, and my country
- yes to my body, my appearance, my health problems, and my physical flaws
- yes to my character, my qualities, and my flaws, and to the possibility of being holier, not by becoming someone else, but by being completely fulfilled
- yes to the trials of my life, the desired and undesired events, the joys, the encounters, and the shifts in my life that have sometimes made me lose my balance but led me to where I am today
- yes to Your love, You who chose me from the very first moment to be Your beloved child
- yes to the mission that You want to entrust me with in this world: whether it amounts to a drop of water or a river does not matter; nobody can accomplish it but me because I am unique

Prayer
On your word depend the consolation of the wretched, the redemption of the captive, the freedom of all the condemned,

the salvation of your entire race, of all the children of Adam. Hasten, then, O Lady, to give your answer; hasten to speak the word so longed for by all on Earth, in Limbo, and in Heaven. Yea, the King and Lord of all things, who has greatly desired your beauty, desires as eagerly your word of consent, by which He has proposed to save the world.[8]

[8] St. Bernard of Clairvaux (1091–1153; Marian Doctor), Homily on the "Missus Est," 2, 4, in *Sermons of St. Bernard on Advent and Christmas* (London: R. & T. Washbourne, 1909), 68–69.

Part 1

Angels, Servants, and Messengers of God

Angels of the Lord, bless the Lord.

—Daniel 3:58

The first mission of the angels, because they are eager and pure, is to contemplate God, sing His praises, proclaim His love, and bring us the fruits of this love. They reveal God's plans, convey His messages, and help us to overcome our small-mindedness so that we can approach God.

2

The Kiss of Fire

I invite you to read this chapter while listening to
The Rite of Spring by Igor Stravinsky in the version
conducted by Pierre Boulez (Deutsche Grammophon).

Isaiah was a man of God in the king's court who tried to bring a morally dissolute and depraved society that was on the verge of ruin back to the faith of its fathers. He lived in Jerusalem in King Ezechias's house in the eighth century BC. He risked his life being a prophet and was eventually assassinated by the king's son.

One day, he saw himself in a vision being transported before the throne of God (see Isa. 6:1–13). He saw the Temple, which was filled with smoke, the six-winged seraphim who were hovering above the throne, the gates that started to tremble, and the Lord, who was seated on His throne. In the face of such magnificence, Isaiah was ashamed and scared because of his weakness:

> Woe is me! For I am lost; for I am a man of unclean lips, and I dwell in the midst of a people of unclean lips; for my eyes have seen the King, the LORD of hosts!

Then flew one of the seraphim[9] to me, having in his hand a burning coal which he had taken with tongs from the altar. And he touched my mouth, and said: "Behold, this has touched your lips; your guilt is taken away, and your sin forgiven."

Thus, Isaiah was prepared for his mission. "And I heard the voice of the Lord saying, 'Whom shall I send, and who will go for us?' Then I said, 'Here am I! Send me!'"

He became God's messenger. "Messenger" is the translation of the word *angel*.

The Power of Words

The biblical text says that the seraphim each had six wings: two to cover their faces, two to cover their feet, and two to fly with (see Isa. 6:2). We call them the "fiery ones" because they are close to God's throne. They cover their faces with their wings because the light that comes from God is so intense. They cover their feet to protect the other angels from the glare that they reflect. This is a little like Moses, whose face was so radiant after he had spoken with God that he had to cover it with a veil (Exod. 34:35).

The seraphim burn with the purest love. We can admire the work of glass blowers on the island of Murano in Venice. They remove the viscous liquid glass from the incandescent fire and give it every possible shape, bringing out its transparence and purity.

"I live among a people of unclean lips": Isaiah could have said a people of unclean hands or eyes. It is through the mouth that we first contact life in our mothers' wombs by swallowing

---

9   The seraphim are the highest in the hierarchy of angels. See the presentation of the hierarchy of angels in the appendix.

the amniotic fluid. This is true even if, of course, the infant's sense of touch is aroused as well through his skin when he moves against the uterine walls. Scientists also tell us that the sense of hearing is aroused very early and that the infant hears his mother's heartbeat and outside noises—especially low sounds. He tastes the world's flavors through his mouth. Doctors have, in this way, observed that in India, amniotic fluid has a strong curry odor. The baby might suck his thumb, and we might see him make faces or smile.

Then the moment of birth comes along, followed by long periods of learning. Communication is established from the very beginning. But the infant will not say his first word until he is twelve to sixteen months old. From that moment on, he will be curious and hungry to learn new words each day, for language is one of the keys to the world and to others.

A toothache certainly reminds us of the importance of our mouths. Eating, speaking, kissing, and breathing: everything converges toward the mouth. It seems that even saliva is full of benefits. Some doctors advise us to create excessive saliva several times a day and swallow it to prevent certain illnesses. If you are really thirsty while hiking, for example, you sense that your tongue is drying up and that you will never be able to speak again! "Let my tongue cling to the roof of my mouth, if I do not remember you" (Ps. 137:6).

The Word Is Creative

We may forget gestures, but we will never forget the words that have wounded us. I have too often hurt my children with words that came out too fast, which I did not mean and regretted.

St. James the apostle warned us to be wary of the power of our words: "No human being can tame the tongue—a restless evil, full of deadly poison. With it we bless the Lord and Father, and with it we curse men, who are made in the likeness of God. From the same mouth come blessing and cursing" (James 3:8-10).

St. Frances of Rome saw her guardian angel in the form of a nine-year-old child. His hair fell on his shoulders in golden curls. He was dressed in a white tunic lined with azure blue and purplish red. His feet remained very clean, even when they stepped in the mud on the paths that he walked on.

One day, when she was with friends, Frances heard some slanderous words that made her uneasy. But she did not dare to intervene. Suddenly, she and her friends heard a noise in the room that sounded like a slap. The young girls looked at each other. They were dumbstruck when they saw Frances's cheek redden, as if she had received a slap in the face. Her guardian angel had used a strong method, according to the educational customs of the day, to silence the viper's tongue!

The holy Curé of Ars tells us that St. Frances continually saw her guardian angel in the figure of an incomparably beautiful child whose face was so resplendent that Frances often read her Divine Office during the night by the light that his face reflected. Her angel was so careful to lead her to perfection that if, at times, she let herself indulge in useless thoughts in her solitude, or if some pointless word escaped her while talking, this good angel made her know her fault by disappearing. She felt very confused and sad for having driven her faithful guardian away. She cried bitterly, asking God to have mercy on her and promising Him that she would mend her ways. After crying for a while, she saw her guardian angel reappear and told him about the pain she has felt for forcing him to withdraw from her.[10]

---

[10] Homily of the Curé of Arts for the feast of the Guardian Angels.

Angels help us to think before speaking—to hold back the word that kills, humiliates, and denigrates! Oh, the hurtful irony that sinks a knife in the heart of its target! Yes, we more easily forget a slap in the face than an insult, for words continue to undermine us. They dig something like an underground river in the depths of our being.

In the film *In Safe Hands*,[11] the people who tend to an abandoned child—doctors, social workers, and the adoptive mother—talk to him for a long time and explain the situation to him. He is upset because his biological mother has left him without a word, so they send for a social worker who met the young mother so that she would explain what she understood about this maternal attitude toward the child.

Mothers have for a long time known the importance of surrounding their children with tender words, songs, commentaries, and little things from everyday life. But, historically, fathers, for the most part, did not tend to talk to young children, who could not respond to them. Their relationship with their children developed only when the children were older and able to communicate.

A Jewish story illustrates the creative power of words. A man named Moshé was trying to take a nap, but some children who were playing under his windows were preventing him from falling asleep. He thought up a story to make them leave and called out to them: "Children, they are givine away falafels at the Damascus Gate. Go get some!"

The children obeyed him. Despite the silence that ensued, Moshé tossed and turned in his bed without being able to sleep.

---

[11] French film by Jeanne Herry, with Sandrine Kiberlain, Gilles Lellouche, and Elodie Bouchez (2018).

"What is bothering you now?" his wife asked.

"To think they are giving away falafels at the Damascus Gate, and I am lying here, trying to sleep!"

Asking Questions

What strikes us in the Bible is that the angels answered the questions that were asked. Who are you? What do you want from us? How is this going to be done? Where must I go? No question repelled or upset them. They responded patiently and politely.

We find only one incident in which an angel got angry (Luke 1:8–22). When the angel Gabriel appeared to Zechariah to tell him about the miraculous birth of John the Baptist, the Messiah's forerunner, Zechariah responded: "How shall I know this? For I am an old man, and my wife is advanced in years." The angel of the Lord gave him the sign that he asked for, but in a rather unexpected way: "Behold, you will be silent and unable to speak until the day that these things come to pass, because you did not believe my words, which will be fulfilled in their time." God's messenger reads people's hearts. In Zechariah's heart, he could have seen years of suffering and possible bitterness, his wife's infertility, the shame before the whole village, the dashed hopes, the prayers that were said to no avail, and the fear of the absence of God in his life. He condemned him to silence. During those nine months, Zechariah meditated on the angel's words in his heart.

In Judaism, people do not give ready-made answers, as with catechisms in the Catholic Church. For example, when little Bernadette of Lourdes, at age fourteen, saw the Virgin Mary, she was still not permitted to make her first Holy Communion because she could not answer the test questions. These were questions that she had to memorize in French, but she understood only the

Bigourdan dialect. The Holy Virgin spoke to her in her dialect. The delicacy of love! But the Jewish people were trained to know how to ask questions. A good question contains the answer in itself. It clears the way and allows a person to see more clearly.

Asking questions is also a sign of confidence. It enables us to understand, know, and love a person better. If it is not a matter of an unhealthy and indiscreet curiosity—we are sometimes uneasy when people question us before this trust is established—we like to be questioned because we enjoy talking about ourselves, even if it is difficult at times.

Coaching, when it has to do with a well-formed professional, brings out the solution that is in us via questions that are skill-fully oriented. Far from "This is what you must do," it is about getting to "I know what I must do. I understand."

Words Go out the Window, Writings Remain

Hagiographers, who study the lives of the saints, wonder how their successors will immerse themselves in the writings of the people whose holiness will have to be evaluated. Which of our text messages will remain? Will it be necessary to comb through Facebook's history?

The writer George Sand left us with more than forty thousand letters! Voltaire wrote more than fifteen thousand, Madame de Sévigné, fifteen hundred, and Cicero, who died in 43 BC, more than nine hundred letters. These are precious testimonies about their eras. Future generations will have to be satisfied with You-Tube videos and selfies to learn about our society. If social media posts do not give them an accurate idea of the way we think, at least they will know what food we ate each hour of the day.

At the end of his Gospel, St. John told us that he could not tell us everything: "There are also many other things which Jesus did; were every one of them to be written, I suppose that the world itself could not contain the books that would be written" (21:25). But, fortunately, the four evangelists took the trouble to recount some of Jesus' actions, including those they experienced and those they heard about.

In the film *My Afternoons with Margueritte*,[12] Germain discovered that books open doors to the world and to others. He was denigrated by his mother, who rejected him but whose love he discovered after her death through her will. He was deeply hurt by a cynical teacher who made his classmates laugh at his expense. (Let us never minimize the importance of teachers in the experience of children and young people.) Germain rediscovered himself, thanks to the respectful and sincere friendship of an elderly lady who read Camus to him and gave him the keys to understanding. These keys are buried but can be found if we dig for them.

The Bible reveals the secrets of the love of God, who plays hide-and-seek with us so that we might be free to find Him. He drops hints, as in a treasure hunt, throughout the Bible. Will we know how to find them?

Love That Travels

The modern troubadour Georges Moustaki described in a 1969 song the death of a young mailman, who condemned the love relationship:

> Love can no longer travel.
> It has lost its messenger....

---

[12] A 2010 French film by Jean Becker with Gérard Depardieu and Gisèle Casadesus.

I love you as much as I ever loved you,
But I cannot say it now.
He carried off with him the last words
that I wrote to you. . . .
Everything now is finished for both of us.[13]

Angels are messengers between God and men. But sometimes they are also messengers of their protégés. St. Gemma Galgani, a young Italian woman who was born in 1878, began seeing her guardian angel when she was seventeen. The first meeting took place when Gemma was getting ready to go out. She was joyfully thinking about wearing the pretty gold watch and chain that was given to her. "The heavenly spirit, looking at her severely, slowly said these words: 'The only jewelry that embellishes the spouse of a crucified King are thorns and the cross.' And he disappeared."[14] Gemma removed the jewelry, fell on her knees, and, crying, made this promise: "For Your love, O Jesus, and to please only You, I promise You that I will never wear any object that feels vain, and I will never talk about it." In spite of her rich family's criticism, Gemma never wore jewelry again and dressed very simply.

Then she was sick for a long time. The angel came to comfort her throughout her illness. She saw him as a handsome adolescent. He looked at her severely when she spoke thoughtlessly or misbehaved at Mass, but he gave her a big smile when she left the confessional. One day, when she was feeling bad, the angel

---

[13] "The Mailman," from the album *The Immigrant* (Polydor, 1969).
[14] This quotation and the following ones are taken from R. P. Germain's book *Gemma Galgani, La Séraphique Vierge de Lucques* [Gemma Galgani, the seraphic virgin of Lucques] (Paris: Brunet-Mignard, 1912).

gave her a little cup of coffee. She said in her autobiography that "the coffee was so good that I was instantly healed."

It was so natural for her to see her angel that she had not thought about mentioning it to her spiritual father, Fr. Germain. People saw her having conversations with her angel. "Gemma saw him with her physical eyes, touched him with her hands—like a human being. She conversed with him, as with a friend.... She spoke with him in the same way that she would with any friend. She gave him endless errands of all kinds to aid earthly inhabitants and communicate with heavenly ones, with a respect that was very humble but full of loving familiarity.... Most of the time, Gemma and the angel prayed together or praised the Most High God."

When she wanted to confide in Fr. Germain but it was not possible for her to leave the house, or if she did not have any stamps, she handed her letter to her guardian angel, who brought it to the priest. She even wrote to Jesus and Mary! Her spiritual father testified to this after her death: "Gemma handed various messages to [her guardian angel] for God, the Blessed Mother, and her holy advocates. She even gave him sealed letters for them, along with the request to bring back responses in their time. It is wonderful that these letters were really carried off by an invisible being. After taking every precaution to assure myself of a supernatural reason for their disappearance, I had to remain convinced that, with regard to this point, as with many others that were less phenomenal, those in Heaven liked to play, so to speak, with a child whose simplicity was so endearing to them."

In the evening, when Gemma went to bed, she asked her angel to trace a cross on her forehead and watch over her. Then she peacefully went to sleep. In the morning, she woke up to go to Mass and declared to her angel, whom she still found at her bedside table: "I have something much better than you. I am going to Jesus."

When her angel left her, he always very gracefully said good-bye to her, and Gemma responded: "Farewell, dear angel. Greet Jesus for me."

Fr. Germain reported that she often had this dialogue with her angel:

"Dear angel," she said, "how much I love you!"

"And why?" He asked.

"Because you teach me to be good, to stay humble, and to please Jesus."

Finally, let us keep the good Fr. Germain's advice in mind: "Do not envy her. For we also have received an angel to look after us from the same Heavenly Father. And if, like Gemma, we are very pure, humble, simple-hearted, and full of faith and holy desires to be perfect, we will be surrounded by as much concern and love."

"Send Me Your Angel"

Later, we will talk more about St. Pio of Pietrelcina. But here is a preview of his relationships with the angels. Sometimes he seemed very busy while he was alone: he was receiving the guardian angels of his spiritual children who were coming to bring him their messages!

Padre Pio often advised those who lived far from the monastery: "Do not move if you have something to tell me, but send me your angel! He does not pay for any train tickets."

When one of his penitents skeptically asked him if he had received her guardian angel's message, he replied sharply, "What do you think? When you send him, he comes. He is more obedient than you!" And he repeated, word for word, the message she wished to send him.

One of his friends asked him, "Do you really hear what I tell you through the intervention of my guardian angel?" The holy priest responded, "So, you think I am deaf?"

At times, he complained because the angels bothered him at all times of the day. "You are rascals! Even at night, you do not leave me alone!"

One day, he even advised someone, "Do not send him to me to tell me foolish things!"

A busload of pilgrims was traveling by night to go and meet Padre Pio. Suddenly, while they were still far from their destination, the vehicle was caught in a frightening storm. Recalling the priest's advice, the pilgrims started praying to Padre Pio's guardian angel. Soon the storm let up. When they arrived at San Giovanni Rotondo, before they could say anything, Padre Pio, who was waiting for them, cried out to them, "My children, you woke me up last night. I had to pray for you."

Another time, when Padre Pio heard it said of someone, "Alas, she is alone," he declared, "Nobody is alone! There is a guardian angel for every person."

Roses or Toads

Do you remember the Charles Perrault tale about two sisters?[15] One was pleasant and helpful, and the other was egotistical and sour. They met a fairy at a fountain. One sister received the blessing that her words would be changed into roses, pearls, and

---

[15] Charles Perrault, "Les Fées" [The Fairies], from the collection *Les contes de ma mère l'Oye* [*Mother Goose Tales*] (1697).

diamonds. The other received the curse that serpents and toads would come out of her mouth.

This rather cruel illustration (like every tale) of the power of words shows us that none of our words are insignificant, just as in the Word of God. "So shall my word be that goes forth from my mouth; it shall not return to me empty, but it shall accomplish that which I purpose, and prosper in the thing for which I sent it" (Isa. 55:11).

Therefore, angels bring us the Word of God and help us to receive it in our hearts so that we can experience it. They touch our "impure lips" with the flame of their love and help us, like St. Dominic, "to speak only of God or with God"!

Prayer

And so, in your presence are countless hosts of Angels,
who serve you day and night
and, gazing upon the glory of your face,
glorify you without ceasing.
With them we, too, confess your name in exultation,
giving voice to every creature under heaven,
as we acclaim:
Holy, Holy, Holy Lord God of hosts.[16]

---

[16] Preface of Eucharistic Prayer IV.

3

The Shepherd's Walk

I invite you to read this chapter while listening to
the *Pastoral* Symphony (Symphony no. 6 in F major),
by Ludwig van Beethoven, this lover of nature
who said that he loved trees more than men.

The flocks were returning to the stable, bleating, trampling, and jostling. The animals were full of lush grass and were worn out by the trek among the rocks. It would be good to nestle in the warm straw. The man at the gate watched them come in. He saw each one in its uniqueness, despite the hustle and bustle.

The silent, invisible angels were watching all around them. They sent discreet signals to the shepherd, who felt confused and uneasy. Even after the sheep were all sheltered, the man felt very anxious. Something was not right tonight: one sheep was missing. He had seen the place where the rebel was tarrying and eyeing a green field whose dangers she did not perceive. But she would have to wait until dawn, he had thought. He must lead the rest of the flock back.

He had already walked so much today, but this thought did not occur to him now. Knowing that she was out there, alone and scared, made him forget his fatigue.

"I must go back," he explained to the well-behaved sheep in the sheepfold. "At any rate, I would not be able to sleep, knowing that she is lost! I cannot abandon her! And I am not abandoning you by going to look for her. I am proving to you that you matter to me and that each of you is precious to me. I need your trust!"

Their peaceful looks responded by saying "Go, we will wait for you all night, if necessary."

He rushed into the darkness, carried by the love that gripped his heart. Was she wounded? A light rain started to fall. She must be cold. Taking long strides, he arrived at the place that seemed so attractive when it was seen from above. But it hid some deep holes, brambles, and sharp rocks.

"Where are you? It is I! I have come to look for you! I will not return without you!"

The invisible, silent angels watched all around him. *Over here, over here!* It was a peaceful intuition—the irrational wish to turn to his right—that directed the shepherd.

A weak bleating of shame and relief rose from the crevice of a rock. He finally saw her, the careless thing, snagged in the thorns that were keeping her imprisoned, and trembling with cold and fear. He freed her. It hurt a little when he pulled on her tangled fleece, but she made no sound. She looked at him with amazement. So he had come for her, leaving all the others in the isolated stable. He could have waited until daybreak! What a good lesson to let her manage on her own! "She wanted to show off. Too bad for her. He had warned her. If the wolf or the lion had devoured her—my word, she would really have had it coming. It was not for lack of warning."

No, he came, setting out at night and struggling through brambles and darkness because it was intolerable that only one was missing. He held her on his knees and rubbed her to warm her up. She laid her head against him. "Forgive me. Thank you."

As she trembled on her hoofs, he lifted her and put her on his shoulders.

"Let us return now."

From the shepherd's shoulders, she now saw the thousand excessively seductive traps of this pasture. At this level, she understood the multiple faces of love—severity, obliviousness, anguish, and anger—that a person shows when he sees a loved one move toward the paths where death lurks.

A glow pierced the night. In the stable, the silent, invisible angels were watching over everything. The sheep made a place among themselves for the survivor and welcomed her on the warm straw.

"Come, little sister; come warm yourself up by us. We have missed you."

There was joy in the stable and all around when the shepherd returned the one that was lost to her peers. Jesus told us: "There is joy before the angels of God over one sinner who repents" (Luke 15:10).[17]

Fatigue and Depression

I am tired. This is perhaps the sentence that we hear the most today. We go to bed tired, we wake up tired, and we drag our fatigue to work, into the family, and to church. Our society suffers from a frantic activism and chronic fatigue. We must run at the risk of being suddenly stopped by *burnout!* Moreover, according to the psychiatrist Christophe André, one in five French people has experienced a bout of depression.

---

[17] Read the parable of the lost sheep in Luke 15:4–7.

Perhaps we are exhausting ourselves without seeing the goal or understanding the meaning of our journey or of life. The athlete who runs in order to score the winning goal no longer feels his fatigue. The mother does not hesitate to be on time when school gets out. A motivation that is greater than fatigue gives them wings.

Léon Bloy said: "There is only one fatigue—the sinful one."[18] Monks have a word for this loss of taste, meaning, and reason for being: *apathy*. They encourage the clergyman who suffers from apathy to plunge back into the very heart of his call. He is urged to pray more and immerse himself in the love of God, for which he came to the monastery in the first place, with his heart burning and his soul at peace.

In the married life, the professional life, and the religious life, there are times of crisis and trial that bring us back to the heart of our call—to the *why* that gives full meaning to what we experience. This is what God criticized in the Church at Ephesus: "I know you are enduring patiently and bearing up for my name's sake, and you have not grown weary. But I have this against you, that you have abandoned the love you had at first. Remember then from what you have fallen, repent and do the works you did at first" (Rev. 2:3–5). Your first love! What has happened to that heart or that fire that runs in the veins and those stars in your eyes?

Lukewarmness has overwhelmed us. Dullness has taken the place of enthusiasm. The well is blocked, and we think that the spring is dried up.

---

[18] Frédéric Chassagne, *Prier 15 jours avec Léon Bloy* [Praying 15 days with Léon Bloy] (Bruyères-le-Châtel: Nouvelle Cité, 2018), 61.

Without Taking Anything

We have to see and measure the immediate fruit of our efforts. "We have worked all night long but have caught nothing." This is what the Galilean fishermen complained about to the young man who had told them to let down their nets.[19] Nobody likes to get tired for no reason. How many of us, after an exhausting but fruitful day, feel a renewed sense of strength to celebrate the victory? Failure, on the other hand, overwhelms us with gloom.

We want to gather the immediate and abundant fruit of what we do for the Church, for Jesus, for others, and even for ourselves when we make a good decision, such as taking up a sport or quitting smoking. This reminds me of a famous comeback:

"Why would they not want my help?"

"Because they don't like you! I don't like you.... Nobody likes you!"[20]

We sometimes experience the same situation in our parishes, prayer groups, and families. Why do they not want my help, my talents, my competence, my ideas, my voice for the choir, my flowers for decoration, my ease in reaching out to others, or my biblical knowledge for the times when the Word of God is shared?

We sow, work, become tired, and do not see the results. Fr. Cencini, an Italian monk, tells us that the most important thing is to sow at all times and in all places, regardless of the harvest.

[19] Read the account of the miraculous catch of fish and the call of the first apostles in Luke 5:1–11.
[20] In the film *Rush Hour*, an American police comedy by Brett Ratner, 1998.

For we are not the ones who reap. "At the end of the day, this believer will wonder if he has sown and not if has reaped.... And he will not know that sowing is already reaping."[21]

The time of hope stretches out between the moment we sow and the day we reap. It is a fragile and beautiful hope that is "flickering in the breath of sin, trembling in all the winds, and anxious at the slightest breath." But it is "as faithful, upright, pure, invincible, immortal, and impossible to extinguish as this little sanctuary flame," according to the words of the poet Charles Péguy. Jesus explained to His disciples the parable of the good seed and the weeds, which He had just told the crowds:

> He who sows the good seed is the Son of man; the field is the world, and the good seed means the sons of the kingdom; the weeds are the sons of the evil one, and the enemy who sowed them is the devil; the harvest is the close of the age, and the reapers are angels. Just as the weeds are gathered and burned with fire, so will it be at the close of the age. The Son of man will send his angels, and they will gather out of his kingdom all causes of sin and all evildoers.... Then the righteous will shine like the sun in the kingdom of their Father. (Matt. 13:37–43)

The Well in the Desert

Hagar, who descended from Egyptian nobility, followed Abraham as a servant of his wife, Sarah. Sarah, being sterile, advised Abraham to conceive a son with Hagar. But when Sarah miraculously gave birth to Isaac, she felt jealous toward Hagar and ordered

---

[21] Amedeo Cencini, *Evangéliser notre sensibilité pour apprendre à discerner* [Evangelizing our sensitivity to learn to discern] (Paris: EdB, 2019).

Abraham to chase away her and her son, Ishmael. Hagar left with some bread and a flask of water and wandered in the desert. When they had drunk all the water, she put the child under a bush, moved away to sit down, and cried: "Do not let me look on the death of the child." An angel called her: "What troubles you, Hagar? Do not be afraid; for God has heard the voice of the boy. Come, lift up the boy and hold him fast with your hand, for I will make a great nation of him." Then Hagar saw a well, filled up the flask, and made her child drink.[22]

In the ninth century BC, the prophet Elijah fled Queen Jezebel's anger. She wanted to put him to death. After a day of walking in the desert, he went to sleep in the shade of a bush and asked God to let him die. "An angel touched him and said to him, 'Get up and eat.'" He looked, and there at his head was a cake baked on hot stones, and a jar of water. He ate and drank and lay down again. The angel of the Lord came a second time, touched him, and said: "Get up and eat, otherwise the journey will be too much for you." He got up and ate and drank; then he walked in the strength of that food for forty days and forty nights to Horeb, the mountain of God. There he received a visit from God — not in a hurricane or an earthquake, but in the rustle of a light breeze. Then Elijah was sent on a mission to those who had not adored the false god Baal.[23]

Hagar and Elijah, who both resigned themselves to dying in the desert, were saved by angels, who restored meaning to their lives. For Hagar, it was the hope that her son would be saved. For Elijah, it was a great mission. When we have a goal and vision of the future that awaits us, we regain all our energy

[22] Read Genesis 21:14–19.
[23] Read 1 Kings 19:4–15.

to attain that goal. This is what Dr. Viktor Frankl, a neurologist and psychiatrist, understood during his stay in a concentration camp. As a deportee in Auschwitz, he observed that those who survived were not the strongest, the most intelligent, and even less, the richest. They were the ones who had the vision of a future — those who saw themselves leaving the camp. "Facing the absurd, the most fragile ones had developed an inner life that left them room to keep hoping and to question the meaning of their lives." After the war, Frankl created logotherapy. "When we find a meaning in the events of life, suffering diminishes and mental health improves." Boris Cyrulnik, a French neuropsychiatrist, spoke about resilience — this capacity to start over after a trauma or a shock.

To get out of a situation we have become entangled in, it is sometimes enough to take a fresh look at our life and to see what was hidden in it until then. It could be a close family member who is counting on us, a mission to accomplish, a goal to attain, or a dream to achieve. Angels help us to see further and understand what can help us to progress.

A Single Flock

A shepherd's staff is curved at one end to help him catch a sheep that has wandered away. Sometimes the shepherd also throws stones at the sheep to make it return to him. The Bible gives us the example of David with his sling. When a sheep went toward a precipice, a wolf, or any of the thousand dangers of the wilderness, the shepherd took drastic steps to make it come back. When life's events knock us down, we complain and blame God for having punished or abandoned us. But weren't we in the act of going toward the void? For the poet Charles Péguy, the shepherd's worry is the beginning of hope:

Jesus, as a man, knew about human worry because a sheep did not come back to the sheepfold and was going to miss the evening call. As a man, Jesus knew what worry in the very heart of charity was—a gnawing charity in the heart of such a dubious charity. But He knew also, thereby, the very first peak of the surge of hope. This is when the young virtue of hope starts to grow in man's heart—under the rough bark—like the first bud in April.[24]

For the Church Fathers, the ninety-nine sheep that stayed in the sheepfold while the shepherd left to look for the lost sheep are angels! This is not because God loves them—His firstborn—less, but because they no longer need to be saved. They already chose to be lost or saved.[25] The dice are cast for them. The sheep have remained with their shepherd. They are going to help Him find those who are missing the call. These include those whose place has remained empty in the fold and those who are still wandering in the wilderness of despair, senselessness, and loneliness.

Jesus told us: "I have other sheep, that are not of this fold; I must bring them also, and they will heed my voice. So there shall be one flock, one shepherd" (John 10:16). When we join the angels and are all reunited in the shelter of the Good Shepherd, there will be much joy in Heaven.

Prayer

My good angel, companion, master, tutor, lord, king, dear and kind prince, who watches over me with so much

---

[24] Charles Péguy, "Le mystère du porche de la deuxième vertu" [The portico of the mystery of the second virtue], in *Oeuvres completes de Charles Péguy*, vol. 5 (NRF, 1916).

[25] For more clarifications on this subject, see the appendix.

Encounters with Angels

goodness, and in whom I have so much confidence, which I will never have enough of, and who supports me in each moment of my life, pray for me.

—Charles de Foucauld

4

The Fiery Encounter

I invite you to read this chapter while listening
to "Spring" in Vivaldi's *Four Seasons*.

It was the fourteenth century BC. Gideon was threshing. He
violently struck the ears of wheat with his flail, as if he wanted
to take out all his rage on them. Would not all this work have
been done in vain if the Midianites came to plunder and crush
his people? What could the tribes of Israel do in the face of this
enemy? Suddenly, the young man was aware that he was not
alone. Someone was sitting under the nearby terebinth. Gideon
perceived in the shade of this majestic tree a marvelous man who
greeted him: "The LORD is with you, you mighty man of valor!"

On hearing these words, Gideon became vehemently angry
again: "Pray, sir, if the Lord is with us, why has all this befallen us?
And where are all his wonderful deeds which our fathers recounted
to us, saying, 'Did not the Lord bring us up from Egypt?' But now
the Lord has cast us off, and given us into the hand of Midian."

"Go in this might of yours and deliver Israel."

Gideon hesitated. Would he laugh or be angry?

"Pray, Lord, how can I deliver Israel? Behold, my clan is the
weakest in Manasseh, and I am the least in my family."

"But I will be with you."

The young man was doubtful. "If now I have found favor with thee, then show me a sign that it is thou who speakest with me."

He killed a kid, prepared unleavened bread, and arranged it on a rock in front of the angel. The angel extended the staff that he was holding. Fire sprang up and consumed the meat and the unleavened bread. With his eyes focused on the flames, Gideon cried out: "Alas, O Lord GOD! For now I have seen the angel of the LORD face to face."

"Peace be to you!" God answered. "Do not fear; you shall not die."

Gideon became a judge and saved Israel from the hands of the Midianites.[26]

God's Signs

Very often in the Bible, the phrase "angel of the Lord" refers to God Himself. He came before His time in the midst of men — incognito, we could say. We have a variation, as in this passage from the book of Judges. The angel of the Lord was seated under the terebinth. When Gideon questioned him, God responded. Then, when the sacrifice took place, the angel turned up and made the fire blaze up. God hides Himself so as not to dazzle or frighten us. He hid Himself behind the angel and in the newborn baby — God made flesh in the mystery of Christmas.

Life's Details

Gideon asked for a sign from God to verify that he was really in His presence. Jesus criticized men for this tendency to want

---

[26] Read this passage in chapter 6 of the book of Judges.

signs all the time without seeing those that were right in front of them: "This generation is an evil generation; it seeks a sign, but no sign will be given it, except the sign of Jonah" (Luke 11:29). What was this sign of Jonah? The prophet stayed in the belly of a fish for three days and three nights. In this way, he foreshadowed the death of Jesus, who would stay in the tomb before rising on the third day, Easter morning. "Jesus will give this sign, but He will do it at the expense of human logic. It will be the Sign of the Cross—of love pushed to its limit."[27]

Some people assert that they do not like to bother with details. They go straight to the goal while seeing only broad outlines. But sometimes one slips on a banana peel—a little forgotten detail on the sidewalk. Life, love, and work are made up of details—a thousand small details that form a chain that is carefully and precisely woven.

> We must pay attention to details. They sprinkle our lives with small stones to guide us. Brutal people, those who wear boxing gloves, and those who are in a hurry or who scatter the small stones, ignore details. They want things that are heavy, imposing, and flashy. They do not want to lose a minute to bend down for a coin, a piece of straw, or a man's trembling hand.[28]

They want signs and clear responses. "Are You the Christ? If God exists, why do we not see Him? Why does He not clearly reveal

---

[27] L. P. Nicolas Bossu, L.C., and Marion Launeau, *Lectio Divina pour chaque dimanche, Carême et semaine sainte* [Lectio Divina for every Sunday: Lent, and Holy Week] (Paris: EdB, 2020).

[28] Katherine Pancol, *Les écureuils de Central Park sont tristes le lundi* [The squirrels of Central Park are sad on Monday] (Paris: Albin Michel, 2010), 185.

Himself? Why do I not hear Him?" God speaks to us—discreetly but effectively—through His Word, His Son, and in our hearts.

His Word

Pope Francis instituted Word of God Sunday, which is to be celebrated each year on the Third Sunday in Ordinary Time. Its goal is "to experience anew how the risen Lord opens up for us the treasury of his word and enables us to proclaim its unfathomable riches before the world." He explained that "we urgently need to grow in our knowledge and love of the Scriptures and of the risen Lord." We are invited to "share it with all those whom we encounter in this life and to proclaim the sure hope that it contains."[29]

The Bible is, effectively, a treasure of "inexhaustible riches."[30] Perhaps we would appreciate it better if we were deprived of it! This was the case in Eastern countries. I recall the associations that clandestinely delivered Bibles. This is still the case in some Asian countries.

Let us read a passage from the book of Nehemiah (8:2–11). It was the year 445 BC. After a long exile, the people returned to Jerusalem, which had been rebuilt. The first day of the seventh month (or the New Year), everyone gathered together in front of the Water Gate. Ezra the scribe pulled out the scroll of the Law of Moses. On a rostrum that was built for the occasion, he read the Law "from early morning until midday, in the presence of the men and the women and those who could understand; and the ears of all the people were attentive to the book of the law." Ezra read a passage from the book of God's Law. Then

[29] Francis, motu proprio *Aperuit illis* (September 30, 2019), 2, 8, 12.
[30] Ibid., 2.

the Levites translated it and gave it meaning, and people could understand it. "Nehemiah, who was the governor, and Ezra the priest and scribe, and the Levites who taught the people said to all the people, 'This day is holy to the LORD your God; do not mourn or weep.' For all the people wept when they heard the words of the law." This lasted eight days!

Let us rediscover this wonderful thing by listening to the different readings at Mass (Old Testament, psalm, epistle), which highlight one another and converge toward the Gospel, which reveals their prophetic depth. Let us nourish ourselves with this holy Word, which strengthens and consoles us. Those who spend time with the Word of God cannot count the number of times when this Word led them exactly to what they were experiencing at that moment. It is as if it were coming from the depths of time to speak to them personally, here and now, in a way that was perfectly adapted to their present situation.

Here is a personal and appropriate testimony, among many examples: While I was working on this book, I was discussing Jacob's struggle, which I mention in chapter 10, with my daughter. It is a passage that she especially likes. She shared with me a homily that she had heard on this episode. I used it for my reflection. After finishing the discussion, I continued working. My daughter went back to her reading. Some time earlier, she had just started reading the whole Bible—from Genesis to Revelation. "Mom, you will never guess what I'm reading!" She showed me the text. It was Genesis 32—Jacob's struggle!

The psalms astound psychologists. We find all the human soul's recesses in them. In the psalms, depressed people find their depths of despair, drug addicts find the pangs of scarcity, and the sick find their fears of death—and, what is more, they find hope! Let us take as an example Psalm 22, which Jesus quoted on the Cross. It starts with "My God, my God, why hast thou forsaken me?" It describes all the stages of abandonment, which are incredibly close to what Jesus experienced in His Passion. Then, in the middle, it tilts toward hope: "But thou, O LORD, be not far off! O thou my help, hasten to my aid!" (v. 19). "For he has not despised or abhorred the affliction of the afflicted" (v. 24). "And I will live for the LORD" (v. 31, NABRE).

Some randomly open the Bible and ask God to speak to them. But let us not forget that God prefers to reveal Himself in "the whisper of a gentle breeze" rather than in "a hurricane" or "an earthquake (see 1 Kings 19:11–13). He does it, that is to say, in our humble daily lives, which will be brilliantly lit up—in the Gospel of the day, in the Liturgy of Hours, or in the phrase of the day on our calendar. Little Thérèse fed on it every day:

> But it is especially the Gospels that sustain me during my hours of prayer, for in them I find what is necessary for my poor little soul. I am constantly discovering in them new lights, hidden and mysterious meanings.[31]

The angels, who know the Word of God perfectly, help us to discover and understand it: "Then the voice which I had heard from heaven spoke to me again, saying, 'Go, take the scroll which is open in the hand of the angel'" (Rev. 10:8).

His Son

Eight centuries before Jesus' birth, the prophet Isaiah announced "The Lord himself will give you a sign. Behold, a young woman shall conceive and bear a son, and shall call his name Immanuel [God is with us]" (Isa. 7:14). God gave us the greatest sign of

---

[31] St. Thérèse of Lisieux, Manuscript A, 83v.

His presence and love through His Son: "Christ's whole earthly life — His words and deeds, His silences and sufferings, indeed His manner of being and speaking — is *Revelation* of the Father. Jesus can say: 'Whoever has seen me has seen the Father' (John 14:9), and the Father can say: 'This is my Son, my Chosen; listen to him!' (Luke 9:35)."[32]

Jesus makes Himself present in the sacraments in the life of the Church today. Thus, Baptism makes us become children of God and takes us from death to eternal life. "When a man baptizes it is really Christ Himself who baptizes."[33] The Sacrament of Reconciliation, or Confession, cleanses us of our sins and reconciles us with God, others, and ourselves. The Eucharist lets us receive the bread of life — the bread of angels: "I am the living bread which came down from heaven; if any one eats of this bread, he will live for ever" (John 6:51). Confirmation unfolds in us all the gifts of the Holy Spirit that we received in Baptism to allow us to spread the Gospel in words and actions. The Anointing of the Sick is especially helpful in sickness or old age. Marriage and Holy Orders are the two sacraments of commitment. They help Christian spouses and priests to carry out their vocation to the full extent through the choice of a state of life. The Holy Spirit, while acting in each sacrament, gives us "love, joy, peace, patience, kindness, goodness, faithfulness, gentleness, self-control" (Gal. 5:22–23).

Our Hearts

We think that our faith would be stronger and more radiant if we received signs from God to show us, in an obvious way, that

---

[32] *Catechism of the Catholic Church* (CCC), no. 516.

[33] Second Vatican Council, Constitution on the Sacred Liturgy *Sacrosanctum Concilium* (December 4, 1963), no. 7.

He is here and that He loves us. The world asks us: "Where is your God" (Ps. 42:3)? Faith can mean the same as trust! It is this act that consists in letting ourselves fall backward, with our eyes closed and our arms extended, into the arms that are stretched out to catch us.

If we look for God's signs in our daily lives, we will find them! They could be in the song lyrics that respond to a question that we ask ourselves; in the newspaper article that echoes a discussion that we have just had; in the sudden illumination that shows us the solution that was in front of us but we had not seen; in the immediate certainty that we must do a certain thing or that we must not go to a certain place; the dream in the early morning that leaves us with a strong impression; the sentence we wrote without knowing what inspired it and that we reread with as-tonished joy; the friend who phones us at the perfect time; the meeting that we are having with just the right person ... I could continue the list ad infinitum, as God's signs are so numerous. But do we bother to see them? We are often so inattentive to others, to events, and to nature. So, perceiving the passage of the angel, whose touch is so gentle and whose message so light, requires that we extend our hearts' feelers!

Meditation

Dear brothers and sisters, we would be removing an important part of the Gospel were we to leave out these beings that are sent by God, who announce and are a sign of his presence among us. Let us invoke them frequently, so that they may sustain us in our commitment to follow Jesus to the point of identifying with him.[34]

---

[34] Pope Benedict XVI, Angelus, March 1, 2009.

5

Save the Country That Is Yours

I invite you to read this chapter while listening to recordings
of musical selections from *The Red Book of Montserrat*.

The day had not yet dawned. The tension was palpable. Joan,
with her eyes raised toward the ramparts of Paris and the Porte
Saint-Honoré, felt her young heart beat wildly under her armor.
The glory of her victorious ride stopped here. Having been warned
by the divine voices that guided her, she knew that she would be
wounded during the attack on this day, September 8, 1429, and that
Paris, which was in the hands of the Burgundians and the English,
would not be freed. She herself would keep failing until she was
captured during the Siege of Compiègne in a few months. This fight
was not hers. Joan of Arc was not French. Domrémy, her native
village, belonged to the Duchy of Bar, which was joined to the
Duchy of Lorraine in 1419, seven or eight years after Joan's birth.

She firmly held her standard, which she would hand over
to her faithful Jean d'Aulon when the battle started. "Jesus ...
Maria ..." Jesus and Mary, do not abandon your child when the
hour of darkness has struck. She did not need to look at the
design that Hauves Poulnoir painted in Tours. She received it
from the King of Heaven. Christ is seated in the middle. He is

holding the world in His hand. An angel is kneeling on each side. To some, they are St. Michael and St. Gabriel. To others, they are the angel of justice and the angel of mercy.

The night wind ruffled her short hair, which was cut in the shape of a bowl, like the hair of her soldiers. She saw once again the little girl who ran in the fields after the harvesters. She was referred to as the shepherdess who became a military leader. But her father had rarely asked her to take care of the animals. She helped her mother, Isabelle, run the house. Being the second youngest of five children, she participated in the harvests and spun the wool and hemp.

Then there was the call. She was thirteen. She always called them her "voices." But they were also beautiful, luminous, and very tender faces. St. Catherine of Alexandria, who stood up to the emperor and all his scholars, was a martyr in the fourth century like Margaret of Antioch. According to legend, the latter escaped alive, with a cross in her hand, from the belly of a dragon that had swallowed her. Joan also heard and saw St. Michael the Archangel, the leader of the celestial army.

First, she was afraid. Moreover, she had estimated the extent of her task. She was a little thirteen-year-old village girl who had never known any soldiers or important people. She was asked to lead an army to fight the Burgundians and the English, deliver the kingdom of France, and put Charles, the heir apparent, on the throne. Joan was devout and polite but also outspoken. She must have sharply asked the heavenly voice what trick it meant to play on her!

And why her? Why not her brothers Jean and Pierre, who dreamed of taking up arms and would join her in the Siege of Orléans? The gentle but insistent voice told her two or three times to go to France. After three years, she had to obey.

The generals gathered around King Charles VII on the Saint-Roch mound. He owed everything to Joan, yet he prevented her from participating in some strategic decisions. He scorned her and was irritated with her and waited for a chance to abandon her into the hands of her enemies. Was this perhaps because she saw him as weak and shaky? Often, great men do not like those who remind them of their modest beginnings. Charles was ready to renounce the throne and yield the kingdom to the English when Joan appeared, with her energy, enthusiasm, and faith. Only seven months had gone by since she came across Chinon, but it seemed to be an eternity. Come on! We have to march into battle and accept a peaceful heart's defeat, in the same way that we have received the glory. After a last invocation to St. Michael in the depth of her heart, Joan rushed off.

Here are some of Joan's answers to her judges during her trial in February 1431:[35]

People in my home called me Jeannette. Since I came to France — "Joan." I learned to spin and sow. I took care of household affairs. I did not go to the fields with the sheep and other animals.

When I was thirteen, I had a voice from God to help me govern my conduct. The first time, I was very scared. After having heard it three times, I understood that it was the voice of an angel. The voice always took good care of me. I always understood it.

[35] *Le Procès de condemnation et le Procès de réhabilitation de Jeanne d'Arc* [Joan of Arc's conviction proceedings and rehabilitation proceedings], trans. Raymond Oursel (Paris: Éditions Denöel, 1959).

The voice told me to go to France and that I could no longer stay where I was! The voice told me to lift the Siege of Orléans. I replied that I was a poor girl who did not know how to go horseback riding or wage war.

After lunch, I went before the King in the castle [in Chinon]. When I entered the room, I recognized him, among others, because of my voice, which revealed him to me.

[Are you sure you're in a state of grace?] If I'm not, may God put me in it. If I'm in it, may God keep me there! I think that if I were in a state of sin, the voice would not come.

[What was the first voice that came to you?] It was St. Michael that I saw in front of me. He was not alone but surrounded by heavenly angels. I saw them with my own eyes, as I see all of you. When they left me, I cried. I would have wanted them to take me away with them.

The Salvation of Nations

Lord, save Your people, and bless Your heritage.
Grant Your people victory over the enemy.
Save this country, which is Yours, by Your Cross.[36]

Can we pray for a country as if it were a person? Yes, for each country comprises the individuals who make it up. It has its own vocation and destiny.

Our country is the part of creation where we live. So we must take care of what God gives us. Our country is the place where we must accomplish what makes us Christian

---

[36] Chant of the Théophanie Community, according to a Byzantine troparion and Psalm 28:9.

... to love our neighbor. What sense would it make to declare that we love the people across the world, whom we do not see, if we do not first love the one whom we see every day, in whose midst we live? Our Christian life starts where we are. If our country disappoints us, we must love it all the more, for God has shown His love all the more by coming to save us when we were slaves to sin.[37]

The Fathers' Heritage

In the book of interviews entitled *The Jesuit*, Cardinal Bergoglio (the future Pope Francis) recalled the notion of fatherland that characterizes the country where we have our roots:

I really like to talk about the fatherland, but not about the country or nation. The country is, in the final analysis, a geographical fact. The nation is a legal and constitutional fact. On the other hand, the fatherland is what gives one an identity. We do not say that someone who loves the place where he lives is a chauvinist or nationalist, but a patriot. Fatherland comes from father. As I have said, it receives the tradition of the fathers, pursues it, and makes it progress. The fatherland is a heritage of the fathers in the present time that must be perpetuated. This is why those who speak of a fatherland that is detached from its heritage, as well as those who want to reduce it to a heritage without allowing it to grow, are mistaken.[38]

---

[37] "Pourquoi prier pour son pays" [Why pray for your country?], Pèlerinage pour la France de Chinon à l'Île Bouchard, http://www. pelepourlafrance.com/home/pourquoi-prier-pour-son-pays-1.

[38] Francesca Ambrogetti and Sergio Ruben, *El Jesuita. Conversaciones con el cardenal Jorge Bergoglio* (Buenos Aires: Ediciones

Encounters with Angels

The love of country, or patriotism, is informed and received by example. To be convinced of this, we need only mention the recent debates about the French soccer players who did not sing "The Marseillaise" before the French team's games. Major character traits emerge from one's country. We say that Germans obey laws, Italians talk with their hands, the English are distant, and the French are rebellious and nonconformist. But we can run into a rebellious German or a French person who is extremely conventional.

Chauvinism, on the other hand, entails thinking that our country is better than others in all things. Xenophobia, or the hatred of strangers, is the somber face of patriotism. It is the refusal to welcome and recognize as a brother the one who comes from somewhere else. Wars rekindle love of the fatherland, as we feel a greater love for that which we are perhaps on the verge of losing. I spoke of "The Marseillaise." There are other songs that could have been chosen as a national anthem — e.g., "The Song of Departure," which I have always personally preferred to the vindictive "Marseillaise." I find that we are more spurred to action by the love of country than by the hatred of enemies:

> The Republic calls for us!
> Let us know how to vanquish or how to perish.
> A Frenchman must live for her.
> A Frenchman must die for her.[39]

B, 2010). The English edition is *Pope Francis: Conversations with Jorge Bergoglio: His Life in His Own Words* (New York: New American Library, 2013).

[39] Revolutionary song in 1794 that was sung a lot during the First World War.

The Language of the Gospel

In 1546, St. Francis Xavier, the great Jesuit evangelizer, visited the Asian islands in pirate seas. He was on the island of More, which was populated by cannibals, whose language he did not speak.

That is where he probably had the most perilous encounters of his adventurous existence. For the natives had become masters in the art of poisons. They collected severed heads and were fond of human flesh. Francis did not know the first word of their dialect. When he saw one of these barbarians, he only had one language. He smiled at him and kissed him![40]

Each nation has its own guardian angel. He is the one who inspires saints and evangelizers to go and announce the Good News to the nation's inhabitants.

As St. Francis Xavier was going to India, he paid his devotion to the country's holy archangel. While he was still in Rome, an angel who was dressed as an Indian visited him and exhorted him to go to those foreign lands. The Macedonian who had appeared to St. Paul and besought him to go to Macedonia to preach the gospel was undoubtedly that country's archangel.[41]

---

[40] "Saint François Xavier (1506–1552)," Jésuites, https://www.jesuites.com/saint-francois-xavier-sj/.

[41] Henry Marie Boudon, *La devotion aux neuf choeurs des Saints Anges* [The devotion to the nine choirs of holy angels] (Paris: Éditions Perisse Frères, 1832).

Each nation has the right to live in peace and be protected from aggression. But peace is formed by changing hearts. This is why the revelations about countries are always a call to prayer.

The Virgin Mary announced the spread of communism in her apparition on July 13, 1917, in Fatima:

> If people listen to my requests, Russia will be converted, and we will have peace. Otherwise, Russia will spread its mistakes across the world and provoke wars and persecutions against the Church. Good people will be martyred, the Holy Father will have much to suffer, and many nations will be wiped out. In the end, my Immaculate Heart will triumph. The Holy Father will dedicate Russia to me. It will convert, and the world will be granted a time of peace. The dogma of the faith will still be preserved in Portugal.

Marcel Van was a Vietnamese Redemptorist brother. When he was young, he received visits from Jesus, which he recorded in his *Conversations*. He knew only one French saint, Thérèse of the Child Jesus and the Holy Face, who came to see him and called him "my brother." But he received secrets about France from Jesus:

> My child, France is still the country that I love and cherish.... I will re-establish my love there.... I am waiting now for only one thing to begin to establish my love in her: that enough prayers are said to me. Then, my child, my love will extend from France throughout the world. I will make use of France to spread the reign of my love everywhere....
>
> Much prayer is needed.... France!... France! Do you promise to be faithful to me? Have you decided to protect and extend the reign of my love in the world?...

France, the country that I especially love ... hear the call of my love. ... If you repulse my love, what other love could you use to raise France up?[42]

Marthe Robin, the little stigmatist from Châteauneuf-de-Galaure also received revelations about France:

France will fall very low—lower than the other nations, because of her pride and the bad leaders that she will have chosen for herself. She will have her nose in the dust. So, she will cry out to God, and the Virgin Mary will come save her. She will rediscover her mission as the Church's eldest daughter and will, once again, send missionaries into the entire world.[43]

This is nothing compared with what will happen. You cannot imagine how far down we will go! But the renewal will be extraordinary, like a ball that bounces back! No, it will bounce back much faster and higher than a ball![44]

Being the "eldest daughter of the Church" is not a small thing! The oldest child is the one who sets an example, who opens the way and leads others in her wake. St. John Paul II recalled this during his homily in Bourget on June 1, 1980: "France, eldest daughter of the Church, are you faithful to the promises of your Baptism?" France has a holy history. Through Clovis's Baptism on Christmas Day in 496, France officially became a Christian nation. France needs saints! This is what St. John Paul II said

---

[42] Marcel Van, *Conversations: With Jesus, Mary and Thérèse of the Child Jesus*, trans. Jack Keogan (Herefordshire: Gracewing, 2008), 32, 37, 39.

[43] To Fr. Finet, 1936.

[44] To Fr. Yannick Bonnet, 1973.

during the celebration of the fifteenth centennial of Clovis's Baptism:

This great jubilee celebration of Baptism is allowing you to reflect *on the gifts that you have received and on the responsibilities that result from them.* Throughout the centuries, these gifts have assuredly been multiplied many times in all those who became the salt of the earth in your country—in those who made shine, and continue to make shine, the great light of the Christian testimony, the apostolate, the missionary spirit, the martyrdom, and all forms of holiness.... This great jubilee of Baptism must lead you to draw up a vast assessment of the spiritual history of the "French soul." You will surely remember dark times and many infidelities and battles, which are consequences of sin. But you will recall that each time we go through a trial, we are urgently called to be converted and be holy, in order to follow Christ to the end. He gave up His life for the salvation of the world. When the night engulfs us, we have to think of the dawn that will come and to believe that, each morning, the Church is reborn through her saints.[45]

After Babel

The construction of the Tower of Babel is a mythical story (like the beginning of Genesis) that shows us the division of the nations (Gen. 11:1–9). "They are one people, and they have all one language; and this is only the beginning of what they will do; and nothing that they propose to do will now be impossible for

---

[45] St. John Paul II, Homily, September 22, 1996, Reims airport.

them. Come, let us go down, and there confuse their language, that they may not understand one another's speech." What had men decided? They wanted to construct "a tower with its top in the heavens." They wanted to defy God.

Jesus came to reconcile all people: "When the Son of man comes in his glory, and all the angels with him, then he will sit on his glorious throne. Before him will be gathered all the nations" (Matt. 25:31–32). He gave us the Holy Spirit, who, at Pentecost, restored the unity that men had lost through pride and lust: "Are not all these who are speaking Galileans? And how is it that we hear, each of us in his own native language?… We hear them telling in our own tongues the mighty works of God" (Acts 2:7–8, 11).

The Virgin Mary, appearing in Lourdes, spoke to little Bernadette in the Bigourdan dialect. (Because she often missed school due to her asthma attacks, she did not know how to read or write and would not learn French until she was sixteen.) The young girl testified that "she speaks to me in a dialect and uses the 'vous' form with me." She was touched by the sensitive way that the Lady spoke to her. Mary did not order her around or make demands. She spoke respectfully to the little girl: "*Boulet avoue la gracia de bié aci penden quinze dias?* [Would you please come here for fifteen days]?"[46]

Joan of Arc's response to her judges was more direct:

Brother Seguin asked, with a Limousin accent: "In what language are your voices speaking?"

"Better than yours!"

---

[46] Apparition on Thursday, February 18, 1858.

Encounters with Angels

Br. Bernard of Quintavalle, St. Francis of Assisi's first companion, was visited by an angel who helped him cross a river:

The angel, clad in the same guise as a traveler, greeted him with the words, "God give thee peace, good brother."

Now Brother Bernard, considering the beauty of the young man, who with so sweet a look pronounced the salutation of peace, according to the custom of his own country, asked of him whence he came....

And, taking him by the hand, in an instant they were both on the other side of the river. Then Brother Bernard knew him for the angel of God, and with great joy and great reverence he exclaimed: "Blessed angel of God, tell me thy name."

The angel answered: "Why dost thou ask my name, which is Wonderful?" Having said these words, he disappeared, leaving Brother Bernard greatly comforted; so that he ended his journey with much joy, noting the day and the hour when the angel had appeared.[47]

The Country That Is Entrusted to You

A country, like each person, needs to be protected:

Then, watchful Guardian, spread thy wings and
  cleave the air,
haste hither to our home committed to thy care;
drive thence each noxious ill that might the soul infest,
nor suffer danger here to rest.[48]

---

[47] *Little Flowers of St. Francis* pt. 1, chap. 4, EWTN, https://www
.ewtn.com/catholicism/library/little-flowers-of-st-francis--part
-1-5468.

[48] St. Robert Bellarmine, Hymn for the Guardian Angels.

In the Acts of the Apostles, St. Paul is called by the angel of Macedonia to announce the Gospel there: "A vision appeared to Paul in the night: a man of Macedonia was standing beseeching him and saying, 'Come over to Macedonia and help us'" (Acts 16:9).

At first, he thought this angel was a man from Macedonia because of his language and clothes. St. Paul may have even asked him who he was. He responded that he was from Macedonia, without any further explanation. But interpreters think that it was this province's guardian angel who implored St. Paul's help. The early Church Fathers believed that each province and kingdom had its own angel who governed it. This opinion was transmitted from the synagogue into the Christian Church. All of this took place in a dream. But St. Paul, who was filled with the Holy Spirit, easily understood what God was asking him and was well aware of the distinction between this dream, which was sent from on high, and other natural dreams.[49]

This is why it is important to bless countries, regions, and cities! Each nation also has its saintly history, its highs and lows, and its sins and advances in holiness. France was consecrated to God by Mary's hands on February 10, 1638, according to King Louis XIII's vow:

By God's grace, Louis, the king of France and Navarre, to all those whom these letters will see, greetings. God, who

---

[49] Dom Calmet's commentary, in *Saint Bible illustrée et commentée* [The illustrated Bible with commentary] (1840), vol. 14.

raises kings to their throne of greatness, not being content with imparting us with the spirit befitting all earthly princes for the conduct of their people, wished to take such special care of our person and State that we cannot consider the happiness of our reign without discerning as many wonderful marks of His goodness as there were perilous accidents....

Our hands are not pure enough to present our offering to Purity itself [that is the Holy Trinity].... It seems reasonable to think that she who mediated to obtain for us these benefits will mediate on our behalf to give thanks to God....

To this end, we have declared and we declare that, taking the very holy and glorious Virgin Mary as special protectress of our kingdom, we particularly consecrate to her our own Self, the State, our Crown, and our subjects, entreating her to inspire in us a holy conduct and to so diligently defend this kingdom against the endeavors of all its enemies that, whether it suffers the plague of war or enjoys the sweetness of the peace we implore from God from the depth of our heart, it may never depart from the path of grace leading to the path to glory.

In September 1870, while the Prussian army was at Paris's gates, two men, Alexandre Legentil and Hubert Rohault de Fleury, made a vow to build a church in Paris if the capital was saved. Two years later, the construction of the Sacred Heart Basilica of Montmartre began. It would be inaugurated on October 16, 1919. The vow was formulated in this way:

In the presence of the misfortunes that have befallen France and the greater misfortunes that perhaps still

threaten her, ... to make honorable amends for our sins
and to obtain pardon for our faults through the infinite
mercy of the Sacred Heart of our Lord Jesus Christ, as
well as the extraordinary help that alone can ... put an
end to the misfortunes of France, we hereby promise to
contribute to the construction of a sanctuary in Paris that
is dedicated to the Sacred Heart of Jesus.

The Virgin Mary asked for the consecration of Russia in her
July 13, 1917, Fatima apparition. This request would be confirmed
in an apparition to Sr. Lucia on June 13, 1929: "The time came
when God asked the Holy Father to consecrate Russia, along
with all the world's bishops, to my Immaculate Heart, promising
thereby to save it." During World War II, on October 31, 1942,
Pope Pius XII consecrated the human race to the Immaculate
Heart of Mary:

> O Mother of Mercy, obtain peace for us from God. Obtain
> especially those graces which can quickly convert hu-
> man hearts. Those graces which can prepare, establish,
> and ensure peace! Queen of Peace, pray for us; give the
> world at war the peace for which all are longing, peace in
> truth, justice and the charity of Christ. Give them peace
> of arms and peace of mind, that in tranquility and order
> the Kingdom of God may expand.

St. John Paul II renewed the consecration of the world on
March 25, 1984, in the presence of 250,000 faithful and in union
with all of the world's bishops:

> Accept, O Mother of Christ, this cry laden with the suf-
> ferings of all individual human beings, laden with the
> sufferings of whole societies. Help us with the power of

the Holy Spirit to conquer all sin: individual sin and the "sin of the world," in all its manifestations. Let there be revealed once more in the history of the world the infinite saving power of the Redemption, the power of merciful Love! May it put a stop to evil! May it transform consciences! May your Immaculate Heart reveal for all the light of Hope! Amen.

On September 3, 2017, Msgr. Philip Tartaglia, the archbishop of Glasgow, consecrated Scotland to Jesus through Mary in the presence of five thousand of the faithful:

We consecrate Scotland to you: all that we have, all that we love, all that we are. To you we give our minds and hearts, our bodies and souls. We willingly place in your service our homes and our families, our parishes and schools.

Msgr. John Armitage, the pastor of the Catholic Shrine of Our Lady in Walsingham, announced that in 2020, England would once again be consecrated as the "Dowry of Mary," this title that England has held since 1061.

In his magnificent text titled *La messe sur le monde* (The Mass on the world), Fr. Teilhard de Chardin offered all of humanity this prayer to replace the Eucharist that he could not celebrate:

Since, once again, Lord, I no longer have bread, or wine, or an altar in the forests of Aisne, but on the steps of Asia, I will arise above the symbols up to the pure majesty of Reality. I, your priest, will offer You the World's work and sorrow on the altar of the whole World....

One by one, Lord, I see and love those You have given me as a support and delight of my existence. One by one,

I also count the members of this other beloved family that the affinities of the heart, scientific research, and thought have gathered together around me little by little, from the most disparate elements.

Less clearly, but without exception, I mention those whose anonymous flock forms the innumerable mass of the living—i.e., those who surround me and support me without my knowing them, those who come and go, and, in particular, those who, in truth and through error, in their office, their laboratory, or their factory, believe in the progress of things and passionately pursue the light today.

Let us also offer our country and its saints, angels, courageous acts, generous impulses, and moments of greatness to the Father of mercies.

In 1960, Padre Pio, launched a call to "a half hour" of goodness for all people throughout world at the same time:

How lovely it would be if everyone in this world decided to be good—for only a half hour a day, on a mutually agreed-upon day! Only a half hour of goodness in order to experience the joy of being good and of seeing how beautiful it is to live in the Lord's grace—without wars, fights, crimes, robberies, or sins! For only a half hour!

Who knows if, after this half hour has gone by, this captivated humanity, won over by so much goodness, would decide to be good up to the day when it will render an account.[50]

---

[50] Giovannni P. Siena, *Bonjour Pade Pio!* [*Hello, Padre Pio!*] (Paris: Éditions du Vieux Colombier, 1960), 115.

6

Encountering a Child's Pure Look

I invite you to read this chapter while listening to
Natasha St-Pier singing Thérèse,[51] a pleasure to listen to.

Here is the strange dream of a small, four-year-old "rascal."[52]
One night, little Thérèse went out to walk alone in the garden.
After having arrived at the bottom of some steps that led to it,
she stopped. She was overcome by fear. On a barrel in front of
her, she saw two little devils dancing "with surprising agility
in spite of the flatirons they had on their feet." Suddenly, they
noticed the child and stared at her with their blazing eyes. Although she was scared, they were much more frightened than
she was. They went to hide themselves in the nearby laundry
room. Thérèse, seeing that they "weren't so brave," was very
curious. She approached the window to see what they were doing. The poor imps ran from table to table, not knowing what
to do to flee her look. From time to time, they anxiously came

---

[51] Two albums: *Thérèse, Vivre d'amour* [Thérèse, living in love],
from 2013, and *Thérèse de Lisieux—Aimer c'est tout donner* [Lov-
ing is giving everything], from 2018.
[52] St. Thérèse of Lisieux, *Story of a Soul*, chap. 1.

to the window to see if she was still there. They then resumed their desperate race. Later, Thérèse would recall that a soul that is close to God does not need to be afraid of demons, who are driven to flee a child's look.

Love That Is Stronger Than Fear

We are afraid. Now, perfect love banishes fear (see 1 John 4:18). Here is a personal example: I often travel, and I get stressed about problems that I encounter, such as delays or mishaps. But when I travel with my husband, I am perfectly relaxed, and I enjoy each moment. Why? Because I trust him. I know that, together, we will find a solution, no matter what the problem is. He is more pragmatic than I am. Unforeseen events stimulate him. Should I have less trust in my Heavenly Father, who has counted all the hairs of our heads (see Matt. 10:30)?

What strikes us about Thérèse is the great strength that was hidden under her appearance as a fragile little flower. Many people have been discouraged by the first words of her autobiography, *Story of a Soul*: "Springtime story of a little white flower." Is she the same one who, in her second notebook, wrote:

> But above all, O my Beloved Savior, I would shed my blood for You even to the very last drop.... I cannot confine myself to desiring one kind of martyrdom. To satisfy me I need all.[53]

At the end of her life, she wrote:

> He permitted my soul to be invaded by the thickest darkness.... I don't want to write any longer about it; I fear

---

[53] Manuscript B, 3r.

I might blaspheme; I fear even that I have already said too much.[54]

Is she the same one who, when a priest to whom she confided her temptations against faith and hope recommended that she carry the text of the Credo on her heart, wrote it with a pen that was dipped in her own blood? Let us not shorten the name that she chose when she became a nun. She was Sr. Thérèse of the Child Jesus and the Holy Face. She incarnated innocence and the Passion (and passion also). What was the secret of this powerful strength of soul that let her drive away demons when she was four and bear a profound dark night of the soul twenty years later?

Like Sons

In his book *Rich Dad, Poor Dad*, Robert T. Kiyosaki tells us that one of the secrets of his rich father is to behave like a rich man in every circumstance — even if he has no money. Would a rich man do that? Would a rich man say that? Would a rich man react like that? Would a rich man dress in that way? This is very interesting, for it reminds us that what counts, first of all, is our state of mind.

If we were aware, each moment, that we are princes and princesses and heirs of the Heavenly King, how would we behave? Little Thérèse was very much aware of this divine connection. Perhaps it was because she had been her earthly father's little queen. Her amusing wedding announcement, which was made during her religious profession, is in the archives of Lisieux. What trust! How sure she was that she had to live as a child of God from that point forward!

---

[54] Manuscript C, 5v and 6v.

Encounters with Angels

Angels look at us and shake their heads. If they were not so pure, we would see them crack a compassionate smile, noting how we sad creatures get entangled in our problems in our short, humble lives. We are full of ourselves and persuaded that we are immortal. But the angels, while contemplating Love day and night, only love us and want to help us. They try to say: "Look up! Look at the goal and end of your existence—love again and again." Love is what will remain at the end. It is all that we will see when we review our lives in God's eyes.

Does this scare us? On the contrary, it is magnificent! For, if I think about it, my most beautiful moments, the people who mattered the most in my life, and my loveliest memories are all connected to love. Even our bitterest tears have come to us from love—a lost love, a wounded love, or a love that was not shared. Fr. Daniel-Ange asks us: "How could that which is love be judged, when it is Love who judges?"

Our Powerful Allies

When we understand this mystery, what joy there is in Heaven! The angels congratulate themselves. They have understood: he is saved! Of course, he will still fall, for a human being is fragile and fickle. But he will continually get back up, with his hand stretched out toward his Father. "Daddy, I fell!"

Thérèse already lived in the Celestial Court, like a prince in exile whom you can recognize because of his self-confidence and ease in every circumstance. Even incognito, sovereigns are escorted by bodyguards who discreetly and effectively watch over them. Thérèse, as a daughter of the King, also saw herself being escorted by the angels, who never left her. They are guardians of the heart and soul who never interrupt their mission at our sides.

In fact, we need allies in a fight. Do we have allies who will fight for us? Elisha replied to his servant who was frightened by the number of their adversaries: "Do not be afraid, for there are more with us than there are with them." The Lord then opened the eyes of the servant, who saw the mountain covered with horses and chariots of fire all around Elisha (see 2 Kings 6:14–17). They were the celestial angels who were ready to defend their protégés.

When Herod started persecuting Christians and after St. James was executed, Peter was also arrested:

> The very night when Herod was about to bring him out, Peter was sleeping between two soldiers, bound with two chains, and sentries before the door were guarding the prison and behold, an angel of the Lord appeared, and a light shone in the cell; and he struck Peter on the side and woke him, saying, "Get up quickly." And the chains fell off his hands. And the angel said to him, "Dress yourself and put on your sandals." And he did so. And he said to him, "Wrap your mantle around you and follow me." And he went out and followed him; he did not know that what was done by the angel was real, but thought he was seeing a vision.... They went out and passed on through one street; and immediately the angel left him. And Peter came to himself, and said, "Now I am sure that the Lord has sent his angel and rescued me from the hand of Herod and from all that the Jewish people were expecting." (Acts 12:6–11)

On October 13, 1884, at the end of the celebration of a Mass in the Sistine Chapel, Pope Leo XIII froze at the foot of the altar. He stayed there for about ten minutes, looking ecstatic and radiating with light. Then, under the puzzled eyes of the cardinals, he ran up to his office and wrote the prayer to St. Michael, while providing instructions that it be recited at the end of each Mass. He would later explain what happened:

> After Mass, I heard two voices. One was gentle and good. The other one was guttural and hard. It seemed that they came from near the tabernacle. The devil was speaking to the Lord, as in a dialogue. Here is what I heard:
>
> The guttural voice, the voice of Satan in his pride, was crying out to the Lord: "I can destroy Your Church."
>
> The Lord's gentle voice: "You can? Then do it."
>
> Satan: "I need more time and power for that."
>
> Our Lord: "How much time? How much power?"
>
> Satan: "Seventy-five to a hundred years and a greater power over those who are at my service."
>
> Our Lord: "You have time, and you will have the power. Do what you want with that."
>
> Then, I had a terrible vision of Hell: I saw the earth surrounded by darkness. From an abyss, I saw a legion of demons that were spreading out over the world to destroy the works of the Church and attack the Church herself, which I could see being driven to an extreme. Then St. Michael appeared and drove the evil spirits back to the abyss. Moreover, I saw St. Michael the Archangel intervene, not then, but much later, when people increased their fervent prayers to the archangel.[55]

---

[55] Msgr. Henri Delassus, *La conjuration antichrétienne* [The anti-Christian spell] (1910).

Prayer

O Glorious Prince of the heavenly host, St. Michael
the Archangel, defend us in the battle and in the terrible
warfare that we are waging against the principalities
and powers, against the rulers of this world of darkness,
against the evil spirits. Come to the aid of man, whom
Almighty God created immortal, made in His own image
and redeemed at a great price from the tyranny of Satan.
You are the one that the Holy Church venerates as its
guardian and protector. The Lord entrusted redeemed
souls to you in order to introduce them into the celestial
bliss. Beseech the God of peace to crush Satan under our
feet in order to remove all his power to keep men captive
and to damage the Church. Present our prayers to the
Most High God so that the mercies of the Lord will quickly
descend upon us. And seize the ancient serpent, who is
none other than the devil or Satan, to precipitate him in
chains in the abyss, so that he can no longer seduce the
nations. . . . Amen.

—Pope Leo XIII

To My Guardian Angel

Glorious Guardian of my soul,
You who shine in God's beautiful Heaven
As a sweet and pure flame
Near the Eternal's throne,
You come down to earth for me,
And enlightening me with your splendor
Fair Angel, you become my Brother,
My Friend, my Consoler! . . .

Encounters with Angels

Knowing my great weakness,
You lead me by the hand,
And I see you tenderly
Remove the stone from my path.
Your sweet voice is always inviting me
To look only at Heaven.
The more you see me humble and little,
The more your face is radiant.

O you who travel through space
More swiftly than lightning,
I beg you, fly in my place
Close to those who are dear to me.
With your wing dry their tears.
Sing how good Jesus is.
Sing that suffering has its charms,
And softly whisper my name. . . .

During my short life, I want
To save my fellow sinners.
O Fair Angel of the Homeland,
Give me holy fervor.
I have nothing but my sacrifices
And austere poverty.
With your celestial delights,
Offer them to the Trinity.

For you, the Kingdom and the Glory,
The Riches of the King of kings.
For me, the ciborium's humble Host.
For me, the Cross's treasure.
With the Cross, with the Host,

With your celestial aid,
In peace I await the other life,
The joys that will last forever.[56]

[56] St. Thérèse of the Child Jesus and the Holy Face, PN 46 (early 1897)

7

The Summit Encounter

I invite you to read this chapter while listening
to the Kyrie in Gabriel Fauré's *Requiem*.

He spent forty days and forty nights in the desert, without the
glow of the love that pushed Him toward the world after thirty
years of a hidden life. When this retreat time ended, He was
reminded of His humanity. Jesus was hungry.[57] The tempter approached Him, pressed where it hurt, exploited the weakness,
and made it a springboard: "If you are the Son of God, command
these stones to become loaves of bread" (Matt. 4:3).

We do not call him the devil for nothing. He knows how to
talk. If Jesus performed this miracle, He would have given in to
the diabolical suggestion. But if He refused, His divine connection, the very heart of His mission, would be doubted. "Ah, so
You are not the Son of God?"

Jesus replied that one does not live by bread alone but by
every word that comes from the mouth of God. As He would
later say: "My food is to do the will of him who sent me" (John

---

[57] Read the account in Matthew 4:1–11 and Luke 4:1–13.

4:34). The hunger that gnaws is not insurmountable. We can transcend it and allow it to become God's desire in us.

Let us change the setting. Here they were in Jerusalem, at the top of the Temple. "If you are the Son of God, throw yourself down; for it is written, 'He will give his angels charge of you,' and 'On their hands they will bear you up, lest you strike your foot against a stone'" (Matt. 4:6).

The tempter loves to provoke doubt, worry, and mistrust: Will Your God, in whom You believe, save You, as He promised, or will He let You crash to the ground? How can something evil affect You if God is watching over You?

"You shall not tempt the Lord your God" (Matt. 4:7).

Love needs no proof. It involves a big leap into the void without a net. We know only at the end if our trust has been betrayed or honored. St. Paul said that love "bears all things, believes all things, hopes all things, endures all things" (1 Cor. 13:7).

The last confrontation took place on a high mountain that made it possible to see all the world's kingdoms and their glory: "All these I will give you, if you will fall down and worship me" (Matt. 4:9).

This was too much: "Begone, Satan! for it is written, 'You shall worship the Lord your God and him only shall you serve'" (Matt. 4:10).

The enemy revealed his supreme ambition: to take God's place in order to receive the adoration and glory that God alone deserves. Jesus reminded the devil of his condition as a creature: "your God." The One you want to depose is still your Creator, Lord, and Master. As for me, I have come into the world to snatch my frightened children out of your hands and to return them to their Father.

The devil left Him. The very gentle, sensitive angels were there to serve Him. Their luminous joy was a balm that comforted Him.

We Do Not Dialogue with the Devil

This Gospel teaches us a strategy to resist temptation:

Jesus, personally facing these trials, overcomes temptation three times in order to fully adhere to the Father's plan. And he reveals the remedies to us: interior life, faith in God, the certainty of his love — the certainty that God loves us, that he is Father, and with this certainty we will overcome every temptation.

But there is one thing to which I would like to draw your attention, something interesting. In responding to the tempter, Jesus does not enter a discussion, but responds to the three challenges with only the Word of God. This teaches us that one does not dialogue with the devil; one must not discuss, one only responds to him with the Word of God.[58]

Eve naively entered into dialogue with the serpent and *boom!* she fell into the trap (Gen. 3:1–19):

The serpent: "So …"

This "So" was the serpent's first word. We hear it as if we were there. We recognize this ironic, half-friendly, half-cruel, provocative voice that incites us to react!

The serpent: "So, God really told you …"

Then there is this "really" that instills doubt, suspicion, and rebellion in us. We do not need to ask whether God speaks the truth, for He *is* the truth. But our twisted thinking unceasingly leads us to doubt His love.

The serpent: "Did God say, 'You shall not eat from any tree in the garden?'"

[58] Francis, Angelus, March 10, 2019.

This is the tempter's subtlety and cunning. It is to slip a small lie in with the truth and to pervert the truth skillfully by highlighting the prohibition.

Eve could not help reacting: "But no, we can eat the fruit of all the trees except for one."

There you go. We have put our finger on human greed. How many times have we forgotten to see the ninety-nine blessings in our lives in order to focus on the hundredth item, which is the only one we do not have? And how many times have we immediately wanted what God intended to give us a little later, when we were mature and responsible enough to benefit from it? Abraham was not patient enough to wait for God's timing. Since the promised son was late in coming, he thought he was being obedient—in following the advice of his wife, Sarah—by fathering his servant's son. But this resulted in many misfortunes for him, his wife, the servant, and the son.

Being children who are spoiled and in a hurry, we do not know how to wait. To educate is to frustrate; this sounds shocking, doesn't it? We want so much to protect our children from the harshness of life that we don't find the strength to educate them in frustration. Yet it is essential, for everything else is the consequence—e.g., patience, a taste for hard work, and even hope. When we cannot wait, we are unaware of what hope tastes like.

Archbishop Fulton Sheen thought that Jesus' three temptations applied to each one of us today.

- The first temptation consists in "trading freedom for security." We are fully there, with the welfare state and the search for no risk!
- The second temptation consists in replacing "the truth with opinions" and "grace with nature." We, too, recognize

it in widespread laxity and the absence of objective stan-
dards. *It is your truth. Everyone does what he likes.* And so
forth.

• Jesus' third temptation is, for our time, that of "a religion
without a cross. A religion without a world to come. A
religion to destroy religions. There will be a counterfeit
Church.... A world parliament of churches. It will be
emptied of all Divine content.... In the midst of all his
seeming love for humanity and his glib talk of freedom
and equality, [the antichrist] will have one great secret
which he will tell to no one: he will not believe in God.
Because his religion will be brotherhood without the
fatherhood of God, he will deceive even the elect."[59]

Now, Jesus came to reveal His God and our God and, even more,
His Father and our Father.

The devil suggested that Jesus avoid the Cross and escape His
Passion and death. He did not offer Him humanity's redemption
and salvation but power and glory. This last temptation was so
essential that, as soon as the devil left Him, angels approached
Jesus and waited on Him (Matt. 4:11).[60] Through their infinite
compassion, they brought Jesus a gentle reflection of the Father's
tenderness.

He who never sinned and cannot sin submits to being
tested and can therefore sympathize with our weaknesses
(cf. Hebrews 4:15). He lets himself be tempted by Satan,
the enemy, who has been opposed to God's saving plan
for humankind from the outset.... Angels, luminous and

---

[59] Fulton J. Sheen, *Communism and the Conscience of the West*
(Indianapolis: Bobbs-Merril, 1948), 24–25.

[60] In Luke, this temptation is the second one.

mysterious figures, appear almost fleetingly before this dark, tenebrous figure who dares to tempt the Lord. Angels, the Gospel says, "ministered" to Jesus (Mark 1:13). They are the antithesis of Satan.[61]

Christ had to go through the crucible of suffering to redeem lost mankind and return it to the Father's heart. Jesus would say "must" several times:

- This must take place. (Matt. 24:6; Mark 13:7)
- You must be born anew. (John 3:7)
- But how then should the scriptures be fulfilled, that it must be so? (Matt. 26:54)
- The gospel must first be preached to all nations. (Mark 13:10)
- I must be in my Father's house. (Luke 2:49)
- I must preach the good news of the kingdom of God. (Luke 4:43)
- The Son of man must suffer many things, and be rejected by the elders and chief priests and scribes, and be killed. (Luke 9:22)
- I must go on my way. (Luke 13:33)
- I must stay at your house. (Luke 19:5)
- So must the Son of man be lifted up. (John 3:14)
- So that the world may know that I love the Father. (John 14:31)

But this "must" has to be understood in the light of His freedom. Jesus' freedom was complete when He offered it for the world's salvation. The word *must*, therefore, bore all His determination and will to love, which was united to the Father's will. He was

---

[61] Benedict XVI, Angelus, March 1, 2009.

like a man who sees his child in danger; nothing will be able to stop him: "I must go save my son." Likewise, Jesus did not even imagine changing so much as an iota of His mission, as His Father had entrusted it to Him.

Adam and Eve prevaricated about God's way of doing things: the fruits of all the trees, except for one—why? Jesus, on the other hand, taught us, through His obedience—an obedience that is enlightened by love and trust—that all that the Father does is best for the world, each of us, and the Church. God can "neither deceive nor be deceived," as we say in a beautiful prayer. He does everything "wisely and lovingly." So, what should we fear? St. Thérèse of the Child Jesus and the Holy Face wrote that "trust and trust alone should lead us to love."[62]

A Contagion

Evil is contagious. Goodness is also, fortunately! How many times have we seen a crowd make a decision according to their first reaction? A gentleman feels faint in the subway. As long as nobody moves, people look at him and do nothing. If one person steps toward the sick man, talks to him, and helps him, then everyone rushes to assist him! We are not sheep, but we need examples because we are paralyzed by our fears.

In my garden this summer, I was removing the nettles that surround our thin raspberry bushes and are as tall as I am. I had put on big gardening gloves. These weeds are treacherous and insidious. I do not object to their value as plants—it seems that nettle soup is very good—but only to their aggressive invasion of my raspberry bushes. When you tear them off, they easily come out with a small root tip. You gain confidence and willingly

[62] Letter 197.

proceed with what you're doing. Then their long stems wrap around your leg or your bare arm and really burn you. The more you move, the more you discover a pile of deep roots that has taken over the ground.

In the same way, without its appearing on the surface, evil takes over our hearts and instills habits that are harder and harder to root out. This starts with little compromising behaviors and complacency: "Well, it's not serious. It's only for today. Tomorrow I will resume my good resolutions." So there are no little lies. There is no congenial laziness. There are no funny slanders. We sow seeds of nettles—or chaff, to use the language of the Gospel—in the gardens of our hearts.

Luckily, Heaven's gardeners, the angels, watch over our plots of good land. They whisper good intentions to us. They give us the strength to follow them. Above all, they propel us toward the most effective weed killer—i.e., the Sacrament of Reconciliation. We are then treated with so many graces there, while our soil is radically regenerated. *Radical* comes from the Latin *radix*, which means "root."

"Tell me, how do we hear angels, and how do we receive these good intuitions that you are talking about?"

If God Himself reveals Himself in "a still small voice" (1 Kings 19:12), angels wave their trumpets only on important occasions. When they speak to us, it is always with the lightness of a feather, to respect our precious freedom. A tiny discomfort invites you to turn away from the inappropriate action that you were going to carry out. A discreet scruple stops a curt word that you were about to speak. A faint nudge, as if you were being pushed with the tip of a finger, sends you toward a person who is experiencing difficulty. An intimate conviction makes you feel like calling a loved one. These miniscule signs are so gentle and light that we must train ourselves to recognize them. But what a privilege it is when we live with them! We feel as if we are cooperating with the invisible world that surrounds us in a way that is as imperceptible as it is certain!

> Before seeing God, His angels, and His saints, I can, starting with the time of my earthly preparation, listen to their voices and be attentive to their suggestions and docile to their advice. I can already sense what I am going to experience and already *foresee* what I am getting ready to *see*.[63]

St. Ignatius of Loyola gave us the means to discern our angels' inspirations:

> In those who go on from good to better, the good Angel touches such a soul sweetly, lightly, and gently, like a drop of water which enters into a sponge; and the evil touches it sharply and with noise and disquiet, as when the drop of water falls on the stone.[64]

Our Secret Thoughts

Neither angels nor demons can access our thoughts. Only God "searches mind and heart" (Rev. 2:23). They can perceive and understand us. But they are not omniscient. This is important in order to understand temptation. Thoughts of envy that come to us, for example, when we see our neighbor's new car, remain merely thoughts as long as we do not take pleasure in them

---

[63] Fr. Daniel-Ange, *La mort et l'au-delà. Noël éternel* [Death and the afterlife: eternal Christmas] (Paris: EdB, 2012).

[64] St. Ignatius of Loyola, *Spiritual Exercises*, seventh rule.

and, above all, as long as we do not express them. We can, of course, sin through our thoughts. At the beginning of Mass, in the Confiteor, we say: "I confess ... that I have sinned in my thoughts and in my words, in what I have done and in what I have failed to do." Nonetheless, angels and demons remain at the door to our inner selves. So, if we say, "I am envious that he can afford a new car," or if we write it—watch out for the texts that take off quicker than lightning; we should think before writing them—we reveal ourselves to the devil, who is happy to have the last word: "Moreover, he is always going on vacation." We are completely responsible for our actions. We fall by ourselves. But if an evil spirit trips us up, we will have a harder time getting back up!

Our angels cannot figure us out either, even if they know us well. They will see that we are anxious and sad but will be less effective if we do not distinctly call out to them for help and do not explain our problems to them. We can, of course, speak or pray to them "in our heads" and not necessarily aloud. As the holy Curé of Ars said in a homily:

> If our guardian angels were not near us to defend us, we would succumb to all the attacks that the devil gives us. Our good angels make us see the temptation. They inspire us to resort to God, who reminds us of His presence to make us afraid of sin. If we are unfortunate enough to sin, our guardian angels will throw themselves at the good Lord's feet to ask Him to have mercy on us. In fact, after each sin, we ordinarily feel remorseful for having sinned. We promise the good Lord that we won't commit it again. It is surely our guardian angels who, by their prayers, make us deserve this grace.

Count God's Blessings

My beautiful Eve, admit that this tree of the knowledge of good and evil, which you were not allowed to touch, was tempting you for a while! But why did you entrust your frustration to the serpent instead of to God Himself?

Lord, explain to me: Why do we not have the right to eat this tree's fruit? What do good and evil mean? Why can we not discern this ourselves?

Eve, for you, who were rebellious, curious, and in a hurry, the fallen angel seemed to be a more interesting spokesman than the God of love. Incidentally, I have written about the lives of the saints, and I happen to meet readers or, rather, nonreaders, at bookfairs, who tell me: "But no, you know, the lives of the saints bore me. We know that we will never be like them. It is too difficult, and it discourages us."

I can understand that people who are too good seem boring. But true holiness is not at all smooth or tidy. It is fiery and lively! A gentle and calm person will not necessarily be a saint. In order to be fulfilled, he might need to stop being calm and to do things that disrupt his daily life a little bit. It is not that holiness goes against our nature. But we still have to get out of our "comfort zones," to take up an expression that is very much in vogue today. As we sing in the "Veni, Sancte Spiritus": "Bend the stubborn heart and will; / Melt the frozen, warm the chill; / Guide the steps that go astray." The hothead will learn to control himself, the shy person will go ahead of the others, and the hyperactive person will work on settling down.... We will try to find a balance by acquiring the qualities that we are most lacking. It is fascinating work! A really holy person—you know one—is never boring. He is lively, vibrant, radiant, attractive, passionate, and interesting. He listens to you, gets you back on track, and makes you feel like progressing.

Encounters with Angels

For the story ends badly! Eve, what have you gained by listening to the tempter's voice? Suffering, fear, and death for yourself and those you love. You hid from God, who could save you. You were no longer "bone of my bones and flesh of my flesh" for your beloved Adam (Gen. 2:23). You were the guilty one. " 'The woman whom thou gavest to be with me, she gave me fruit of the tree, and I ate' " (Gen. 3:12).

Let us be wary of blanket accusations that seem to justify blame. Many have used the temptation of Eve as an excuse to denigrate women. Violence against women must, of course, be severely sanctioned. There is nothing more revolting than those light suspended sentences that are meant to punish those who murder or abuse their partners! It is not easy to be a woman in the 2020s. If she has some responsibility at work, she has to be the first one to arrive and the last one to leave. She must have all the skills and must never make mistakes. In the family, she must stay thin and pretty, know how to prepare good meals, and wash and put away all the laundry. She must also be available to drive whenever people need to be driven, attend all parent-teacher conferences, and be available to and patient with her children, having incorporated the latest data on the Montessori method and positive education. In doing so, she does not neglect social networks and belongs to many groups where she shares her experience with humor and relevance. I could continue. A thousand constraints, like so many heavy cords, pull us in all directions and tear us apart. We live nonstop in a state of tension that can end up being unbearable.

Yet let us honestly recognize that it is not easy to be a man either. He must be both gentle and strong, tender and sensitive without ceasing to be virile and protective. He also must take care of himself without becoming egotistical, must understand "what women want" while validating his point of view, and finally, must know how to exercise proper authority while being a dad who is shrewd, funny, reassuring, and playful. As the Italian writer Andrea Torquato Giovanoli humorously wrote:

> Once upon a time, man existed. He was solid, virile, and a little rustic, if you wish, but knew exactly what his role was. Maybe he had too many hairs on his back, but few on his tongue. He did not speak a lot. But when he opened his mouth, people listened to him because he was exercising his natural authority. He exaggerated his authority at times because he felt threatened and was trying to mark the boundaries of his territory. Today, on the contrary, man is an endangered creature, just like the panda.... Today's man is refashioned in the image and likeness of the woman. On the contrary, she has become more masculine in everything, if not in aesthetics, at least in her attributes, to the point of confusing the sexes. People can then assert that they do not exist, now that they are indistinguishable.[65]

Who will restore to us the grace of being a man or a woman and the wonder of the first day? Hope is restored to us in the last book of the Bible: "To him who conquers I will grant to eat of the tree of life, which is in the paradise of God" (Rev. 2:7). The garden is closed and guarded by an angel with a flaming sword. But the tree of life is still there, and God has not changed His mind. He wants to offer it to us. God does not go back on His

---

[65] Andrea Torquato Giovanoli, *Le syndrome du panda. Petit manuel de survie pour les hommes d'aujourd'hui* [The panda syndrome. a little manual of survival for today's men] (Paris: EdB, 2017).

promises. Things did not go as they should have. Man has made some big mistakes. This is not serious. God finds a way. He sent us prophets and His Son, who became one of us. He places His divinity within humanity to draw us into His holiness!

After his whims, anger, and roundabout ways, the repentant Adam came back to God and received the gift of eternal life with six thousand years of delay, which is nothing for God. When we desire, time does not count, and God desires us infinitely. "Come, my little one, the voice of the serpent has become silent. All that remains is the singing of the angels, who tell you: return to your home. Come into my arms. I have waited for you for so long."

Prayer

O holy angel, Divine Providence has entrusted the care of my soul to you. Watch always over me. Help me when I am tempted. Present my prayers to God. Intercede for me. Drive away from me all my enemy's temptations. Obtain from the God of mercy what I cannot get for myself. Let the thought of evil be unable to penetrate me. Let it never find a place there! And if I am unfortunate enough to stray from the path where God's hand leads me, bring me back right away, I beg you, into the footsteps of my Savior.

—St. Francis Xavier

Part 2

Angels in the Liturgy

In the presence of the angels to you I sing.

—Psalm 138:1, NABRE

Because they are happy and grateful, the angels' second
mission is to join the Church in the celebration of
the liturgy. They awaken our eagerness and encourage
our enthusiasm. They teach us how to pray.

8

The Glory and the Joy

I invite you to read this chapter while listening to
Vivaldi's *Gloria* in D major. Emotion is guaranteed.

It was a little cold. They lit a fire. The sky was dark and full of
stars. The animals were peacefully resting. Two men were talking
about the census. How crazy! So many families had arrived from
Judea, Galilee, and the distant provinces of the Decapolis that
people no longer knew where to house them. This was going to
end badly. Was it necessary to count men as sheep were counted?
Suddenly, something very bright made them jump. Was it a flash
of lightning or a fire?

A human silhouette was descending from the sky and coming
toward them. They were surrounded by light and paralyzed by
fear. One of them lifted his rod in a pathetic gesture of protection. The angel started to speak:

> Do not be afraid; for behold, I proclaim to you good news
> of great joy that will be for all the people. For today in
> the city of David a savior has been born for you who is
> Messiah and Lord. And this will be a sign for you: you will
> find an infant wrapped in swaddling clothes and lying in
> a manger. (Luke 2:10–12)

He had hardly finished speaking when thousands of angels surrounded him. They were so beautiful and luminous that they took the shepherds' breath away. In a triumphant melody, they started to praise God: "Glory to God in the highest, and on earth peace to those on whom his favor rests" (Luke 2:14).

Time seemed suspended. Then the angels disappeared in the way they had come. The men wondered if they were dreaming. They consulted each other. Did they really hear the same words?

"An extraordinary event that the Lord made known to us took place in Bethlehem."

"What event? And why us?"

"Let's go!"

"Yes, yes, let's go!"

The city was sleeping. But a light shone in one of the area's numerous caves. The shepherds slowly came in and found a man, a woman, a little donkey, and there, in the manger, a newborn who was looking at them and waving His hands while laughing. When they left again, they were so full of joy that they had to share it. They woke the inhabitants to announce the good news to them: "Glory and praise to God! Salvation has entered the world!"[66]

Praise and Heavenly Music

"Where were you," God asked Job, "when I founded the earth ... while the morning stars sang together and all the sons of God shouted for joy?" (Job 38:4, 7).

The angels invite us to sing in praise of creation.

The *Catechism of the Catholic Church* tells us that "the composition and singing of inspired psalms, often accompanied by

[66] Read this passage in Luke 2:1–20.

musical instruments, were already closely linked to the liturgical celebrations of the Old Covenant. The Church continues and develops this tradition" (1156). Many people were converted by the beauty of liturgical chants. For example, St. Augustine wrote:

How I wept, deeply moved by your hymns, songs, and the voices that echoed through your Church! What emotion I experienced in them! Those sounds flowed into my ears distilling the truth in my heart. A feeling of devotion surged within me, and tears streamed down my face—tears that did me good.[67]

St. Hildegard of Bingen, a Doctor of the Church, was not just a Benedictine superior, mystic, diplomat, woman of letters, naturopath, and linguist but also a composer. She left us with seventy-seven liturgical chants, hymns, and sequences and a liturgical drama: *The Order of the Virtues*. Fr. Pierre Dumoulin wrote that these works make up one of the richest repertoires of medieval music. Yet they are not the fruit of a composition work, strictly speaking, but the transcription of celestial harmonies that the saint perceived through her visions.[68]

Hildegard actually contemplated the heavenly myriads. "Some radiated like fire. Others were completely clear. Still others glittered like stars. It was a concert of voices that was like the sound of the sea." She thought that the angel was man's model. The

---

[67] St. Augustine, *Conf.* 9, 6, 14: PL 32,769–770, quoted in CCC 1157.

[68] Fr. Pierre Dumoulin, *Hildegarde de Bingen. Prophète et docteur pour le troisième millénaire* [Hildegard of Bingen: prophet and doctor for the third millennium] (Paris: EdB, 2012).

angel reminded St. Hildegard that praise was her vocation: "Man, God's creature, must praise Him because his soul is made to live in praise, like the angels." The Fall contributed to disturbing the original harmony whose memory lives in us and which we must rediscover: "The canticle of praise is rooted in the Church according to celestial harmony through the Holy Spirit." St. Gregory said it before her: music is the most elevated of all human activities. Hildegard believed that "when man's spirit is well directed, he hears the song of the angels." "The soul is itself a symphony, and it harmonizes everything." She wrote that "the cohort of the angels yearns for God. It recognizes Him throughout the symphony of its praises and celebrates its past and present eternal mysteries."

Gratitude

Do we know how to count God's blessings, as the Bible invites us to do, and look at all that we have received from Him? This includes life, family, friends, health, home, work, leisure activities, and beautiful scenery to look at. Let us not be spoiled children who are never content! In my family, we have, for many years, kept a diary in which we note happy events, parties, anniversaries, and outings, with pictures and drawings. Why not start a "notebook of wonders" to recall what makes us feel good? This could be a phrase that we read or a homily that touched us, an answer to our prayers, a place that left its mark on us, a person who built us up, a teaching, a song ... When the clouds hide the sun or when the hours are slow and gray, it would be a relief to revisit these stretches of blue skies to rekindle our confidence.

It is important to be grateful, for we are owed nothing. Everything is a gift. "Everything is grace." Yet praising is not simply thanking God for His blessings. It is very nice to say "thank you." But praising takes us further:

> Praise is the form of prayer which recognizes most immediately that God is God. It lauds God for his own sake and gives him glory, quite beyond what he does, but simply because HE IS. It shares in the blessed happiness of the pure of heart who love God in faith before seeing him in glory. By praise, the Spirit is joined to our spirits to bear witness that we are children of God (1 Cor. 8:6). (CCC 2639)

We are not only to celebrate the praise of God with our songs but are also to *become a glorious praise* through our whole life, as St. Elizabeth of the Trinity had sensed: "A Praise of glory is a soul of silence that remains like a lyre under the mysterious touch of the Holy Spirit so that He may draw from it divine harmonies."[69] Angels, who never cease praising Him, lead us in this jubilation:

> *Filled with wonder,*
> *we extol the power of your love,*
> *and, proclaiming our joy*
> *at the salvation that comes from you,*
> *we join in the heavenly hymn of countless hosts*
> *as without end we acclaim:*
> *Holy, Holy, Holy Lord God of hosts.*[70]

---

[69] St. Elizabeth of the Trinity, January 25, 1904, "Saint Elizabeth of the Trinity (1880–1906)," Boston Carmel, https://carmelitesofboston.org/spirit-of-carmel/our-saints/saint-elizabeth-of-the-trinity/.

[70] Eucharistic prayer for reconciliation I.

We can thank the angels for all that they are doing for us: "We should be so thankful for all the good services that they render us all times!"[71]

Prayer

O Lord, our Sovereign, how majestic is Your name in all the earth! Your splendor is sung by the mouths of children and infants. (Psalm 8:1–2)

The heavens are telling the glory of God; and the firmament proclaims his handiwork. (Psalm 19:1)

[71] Fr. Jean-Jacques Olier, Letter 385.

9

The Eucharistic Encounter

I invite you to read this chapter while listening
to "Pange Lingua," a Eucharistic hymn composed
by St. Thomas Aquinas in 1264.

It was the end of September, during the feast of the Holy Archangels. St. Angela tells us:

> While I was in the church in Foligno and desired to com-
> municate, I prayed to the Holy Angels, and especially to
> St. Michael and the Angels of the Seraphim, and said:
> "O ministering Angels, who have the power and the of-
> fice from God to administer Him to others, by expressing
> His knowledge and love, I beseech you to present Him
> unto me, such as the Father of Mercies gave Him unto
> men, and as He willeth and hath willed to be received
> and worshipped by us; that is to say, poor, and sorrowing,
> and despised, and wounded, and bleeding, and crucified,
> and dead upon the cross." Then said the Angels unto me
> with unutterable pleasantness and sweetness: "O thou
> who art pleasing unto God, behold, He is ministered unto
> thee, and thou hast Him present; and over and above it

hath been granted thee, that thou mayest present Him and administer Him to others." Then in truth I beheld Him present, and I saw Him very clearly with the eyes of my soul, in the Sacrament, even as I had asked for Him, namely, dolorous, and bleeding, and crucified, and afterwards dead upon the cross. Then, too, I felt so exceeding sharp a pain, that it seemed unto me that my heart would burst by reason of the presence of so dolorous a vision; and on the other hand, I took delight and joy in the presence of the Angels, and never would have thought, unless I had seen it, that the Angels were so pleasing, and that they could give such joy unto the soul.[72]

The Bread of Angels

It is Jacob's ladder — this unheard exchange between Heaven and earth — that appears before us:

Be pleased to look upon these offerings with a serene and kindly countenance, and to accept them.... In humble prayer we ask you, almighty God: command that these gifts be borne by the hands of your holy Angel to your altar on high in the sight of your divine majesty, so that all of us, who through this participation at the altar receive the most holy Body and Blood of your Son, may be filled with every grace and heavenly blessing.[73]

Angels help us to understand this great mystery and to live it.

[72] *The Book of the Visions and Instructions of Blessed Angela of Foligno*, trans. Rev. A. P. J. Cruikshank, 2nd ed. (London: Art and Book, 1888), chap. 38, pp. 137–138.

[73] Eucharistic Prayer I.

"I Am Going to Love"

Before going to Mass each morning, St. Germaine of Pibrac stuck her staff in the ground in the middle of her flock. An angel came to watch over the flock in her place. Despite the wolves that were howling around them, she never lost a single animal.

Likewise, when St. Isidore went to Mass in the early morning while his work companions went to the fields, two angels who looked like sturdy youths plowed and cultivated in Isidore's place until he returned.

Benoîte Rencurel, a shepherdess from Laus, saw angels flying in the air above the tabernacle and around the altar during Mass. "They were laughing as if they were perfectly happy to see the faithful gathered together in prayer." St. John Chrysostom said: "The whole sanctuary and the space around the altar are filled with heavenly powers to honor the One who is present on the altar." He explained that, when Mass started, legions of angels surrounded the altar "in an attitude that is comparable to warriors in the presence of their king."

St. Brigid thought that the cherubim made "the air vibrate with unspeakable sounds and songs" during the Consecration.

Agnes of Langeac, a Dominican nun, never said: "I am going to Mass" but "I am going to love!" One day, her spiritual father prohibited her from going to Communion because of her excessive desire for it. At the end of Mass, he realized that one of the remaining hosts was missing. Then Agnes admitted to him that her angel had come to take a host from the ciborium to give her.

Therese Neumann, like Marthe Robin, could not absorb any food. For thirty-five years, she lived only on daily Communion. Therese constantly saw her angel, who stood to her right and revealed to her secrets about her visitors. She knew if it had been a long time since people who came to see her had received

Communion. She could also tell whether a host that someone presented her was consecrated.

Sometimes angels offer Communion. The angel who appeared to the three children in Fatima gave them Communion. Lucia received the Body of Christ, while Francisco and Jacinta consumed the Blood of Christ. The angel said to them: "Receive the Body and Blood of Christ, and console your God!"

Likewise, Benoîte Rencurel received Communion from her angel one day when there was no priest. He said to her: "I will give you Communion. Light the candles, approach the altar, take the cloth, and kneel." Then he ordered her to go into her room "to pray and thank God."

So Great and So Humble

Are we aware of what we are doing when we receive Jesus in Communion? Sometimes the casual or distracted attitude of some of the faithful can encourage us to think: "Only those who want to receive Jesus, who is really present in this bread, should come forward!" But are we ourselves really present to the presence of the one who gives Himself to us? Let us be fully attentive to what happens in this beautiful moment of the celebration of the Mass. I have sometimes heard people respond with a "thank you" when receiving the host, but the liturgical dialogue is so beautiful:

"The Body of Christ," your Lord and God, your Beloved who gave His life to save you.

"Amen," I believe it. I support this with all my soul. I want it more than anything!

This reminds me of these words from the holy Curé of Ars: "If a single Mass were celebrated in the world, multitudes would rush to it by the millions."

This Eucharistic mystery is so humble that we run the risk of trivializing it as Sundays go by. Yet let us not judge according to appearances, for only God sees our hearts. Who knows if the young person we glare at because he is chewing gum is not carrying a heavy burden that he has just laid down as he received Communion?

Fortunately, the Bread of Life is also the Bread for the poor. Let us not wait to be saints to receive Communion, for Communion sanctifies us! It nourishes in us spiritual forces through which we become more devoted and attentive to others. The Curé of Ars believed that each person who comes to receive Communion is escorted by his guardian angel. Our guardian angels, more than anyone else, can help us to be more enthusiastic and vigilant.

> Lord, You are the Bread of Life.
> You give Your very self to me.
> I receive what I am—the Body of Christ—
> so that I may become what I receive: the Body of Christ.[74]

St. Philip Neri was in ecstasy at each Eucharist, sometimes even from the time he put on his priestly vestments. "His eyes, which were fixed on Heaven, no longer saw what surrounded him." When he received Communion, his heart throbbed and tears flowed down his face.

When Padre Pio celebrated Mass, it sometimes took him fifteen minutes to say the words of Consecration because they led him to become so contemplative. Likewise, when he elevated the host in front of the faithful, he kept his eyes fixed on Jesus for several minutes. Fr. Derobert thought that people did not

---

[74] Based on a sermon by St. Augustine, *Youcat: Youth Prayer Book* (San Francisco: Ignatius Press, 2013).

"attend" Padre Pio's Mass; they "participated in" it. Another priest testified: "The Eucharist was the center of attraction toward which all the moments of Padre Pio's day converged. Each hour of the day was an uninterrupted preparation and a continuous thanksgiving to Jesus in the Blessed Sacrament."

Some priests asked him: "Are we the only ones who stand around the altar during Mass?" Padre Pio said that God's angels were around the altar.

"Father, who is found around the altar?"

"The whole celestial court."

Panis Angelicus

The Bread of angels
Becomes the Bread of men.
The Heavenly Bread puts
An end to symbols.
O admirable thing!
The poor man, the servant, the little one
Nourishes himself with His Lord.
Holy Trinity,
One God, we ask You,
Deign by Your visit
To respond to our tribute.
Lead us through our paths
To the goal that we are aiming for.
To the light where You dwell.
Amen."

—Saint Thomas Aquinas

10

The Struggle and the Blessing

I invite you to read this chapter while
listening to Verdi's *Requiem*.

After having moved his family and flocks forward, Jacob stayed
by himself. He was gripped by fear. Was it not crazy to want to
return to his native land after the bad trick that he played on
his older brother by usurping his birthright and their father's
blessing? His brother, Esau, was advancing on him with four
hundred men.

Suddenly, someone was near him. He made him out through
the light of the fire. Was he a man or an angel? Jacob was familiar
with angels. Didn't they welcome him when he arrived in this
place so that he could camp here? The man grabbed him and
wrestled with him. The struggle lasted until daybreak without
either one of them getting the upper hand. Seeing that he could
not do anything against him, the man struck Jacob on the hip
socket and said to him: "Let me go, for the day is breaking."

"I will not let you go, unless you bless me."

"Your name shall no more be called Jacob, but Israel [he who
strives with God], for you have striven with God and with men,
and have prevailed."

He blessed Jacob before disappearing. Jacob, who continued to limp after the struggle, then called the place Peniel, which means "Face of God," for he saw God face-to-face and his life was preserved.[75]

Some Time for God

"I would like to pray. I know that it is important. But if you knew about my schedule—I do not have the time!"

We continually hear this. I do not have time to exercise. I do not have time to answer you. I do not have time for my children or for God. Yet I have seen the following numbers in multiple polls: those who are thirty-five to fifty years old spend two and a half hours a day on their phones. Those who are fifteen spend six hours and forty-five minutes on theirs! Almost seven hours per day and fifty hours per week that could be used so much better! Okay, it is often while doing something else—while traveling or waiting in line. But if we are sincere, we will see that we do have this time that we are supposedly lacking. We can pray while waiting in front of the school. We can pray in the line at the supermarket or the post office. We can do without music while taking a shower.

All of human history goes through a tough struggle against the powers of darkness. This is a struggle that started when the world began which, according to the word of the Lord, will last up until the Last Day.[76]

In Praise of Weakness

We look for strength and solidity in a leader. Jesus appeared to His disciples to be extremely weak. He was handed over into the

---

[75] Read this passage in Genesis 32:25–32.
[76] Second Vatican Council, *Gaudium et Spes*, no. 37.

hands of men to suffer the long hours of His Passion. He could, nonetheless, have gotten the help of angels. This is what He assured Peter, who was trying to defend him: "Do you think that I cannot appeal to my Father, and he will at once send me more than twelve legions of angels?" (Matt. 26:53).

Many leaders refuse to show their weaknesses, admit their limitations, or recognize their mistakes. But what do we expect of those who lead us? That they be strong, perfect, and infallible? We simply want them, despite their flaws or faults, to lead us, in their zeal, toward a horizon that they perceive better than we do. The leader is the one who has the vision. As long as he maintains this goal, others will be able to follow him with complete confidence. If necessary and if they want to, they will make up for his shortcomings. This is about breaking the shell. The one who exposes himself to his subordinates can either receive their scorn if he tries to justify himself and hide or gain their trust. In either case, there will be no possible going back.

Here is a family example: My great-aunt married the head of a wholesale grocery-supply business, which included oil. He was much older than she was. When he died after a short illness, my great-aunt ended up being the young and inexperienced head of the company. She gathered together all the representatives and told them: "I do not know anything about this. But the future will depend on your decision. Either you will help me, and we will continue together, or I will stop everything. I do not want to pretend to be up to the task. I have everything to learn from you." They all chose to trust her and continue, and the company flourished. She was not afraid to pitch in to drive the vans and deliver the Lorraine spices. This is how she met a grocer from Nancy and introduced him to her niece, who was finishing school and became the company's accounting secretary.

The grocer had a son. The son and the secretary ended up getting married, and this is how I was born.

Narrow, but Open

In a homily on Luke 13:22–30, in which Jesus exhorts us, "Strive to enter by the narrow door; for many, I tell you, will seek to enter and will not be able," a priest made the following remark: "Jesus tells us that the door is narrow, but He does not tell us that it is closed. The door is open. It will not always be easy to go through the door, but it remains open for us."

Whether it was a chance circumstance or providential, Pope Francis developed this idea in his Angelus message on the same Sunday in St. Peter's Square:

> It is a case of taking the right way from now, and this right way is *for everyone, but it is narrow.* This is the problem. Jesus does not want to give us false hopes by saying: "Yes, do not worry, it is easy, there is a beautiful highway with a large gate at the end ..." He does not say this. He tells us things as they truly are: the doorway is narrow. In what sense? In the sense that, in order to save oneself, one has to love God and neighbour, and this is uncomfortable! It is a "narrow doorway" because it is demanding. Love is always demanding. It requires commitment, indeed, "effort", that is, a determined and persevering willingness to live according to the Gospel.... This is why we invoke her as "Mary Gate of Heaven", a gate that traces the form of Jesus precisely: the door to God's heart, a demanding heart, but one that is open to us all.[77]

---

[77] Francis, Angelus, August 25, 2019.

The Grace of Fidelity

The Dominican theologian Yves Congar wrote: "I did not receive the grace of prayer, but I received the grace of fidelity in prayer." Fidelity is a gift, but it is also a choice. Sometimes we need to rely on the will when we don't want to—when heaviness overwhelms us. Keeping everything in proportion, going to Mass, or taking time to pray can, at first, seem like going to the gym. When we get there, we no longer feel like participating in it. We look for a thousand excuses, but when we make ourselves go there, we are so happy! We must keep going, through thick and thin, to get this "hard-won" blessing. Effort, perseverance, and fidelity are hardly popular, but they build our spiritual spine. If we give up because of the first excuse that comes along, what will happen during the big storms? Have we built our faith on sand or on rock?

On May 22, 2019, a month after the big fire in Paris's Notre-Dame Cathedral on April 15, one of the four cherubim that adorned the keystone was discovered in the debris. Three strong symbols escaped the flames and the collapse—the golden cross, a statue of the Virgin Mary like the *Pietà*, and the angel.

A Prayer Companion

Pope Pius XII promised that "our guardian angel does everything he can to support our spiritual ascent and develop our intimacy with God." This is why our guardian angels can help us to pray when we are feeling lukewarm or discouraged.

Padre Pio advised his spiritual children to rely on their guardian angels' intercession to grow in their prayer life:

> This heavenly spirit guides and protects us like a friend,
> a brother. But it is very consoling to know that this angel

prays unceasingly for us, and offers God all of our good actions, our thoughts, and our desires, if they are pure.[78]

The angels' help can even be material. Benoîte Rencurel, the young prophet of Notre-Dame-du-Laus, saw her guardian angel as well as the Virgin Mary. Sometimes, he was a beautiful child with wings. Other times, he was a fifteen- or sixteen-year-old boy. At times, he was accompanied by other angels. At night, when she went up to pray and found the church door closed, the angel came to open it for her. But if he did not come, she stayed on the doorstep.

On Christmas night in 1700, some angels stood near her. While the Gloria was being sung in Latin, an angel translated for her the words that she did not understand.

St. John Climacus thought that we could feel the presence of our angels in prayer: "If, when you repeat a word, you experience interior consolation and tenderness, hold on to this single word, for your angel is praying along with you."

St. Gertrude of Helfta also thanked her guardian angel:

Blessed be your love and all your care, you who do not cease to hasten my salvation! I ask you to forgive me for having so often resisted your suggestions and saddening you in this way, O my good friend. I resolve to obey you in the future and serve God faithfully.

The Simple Prayer of the Rosary

In October 2001, Sr. Lucia of Fatima wrote to all the world's Marian communities:

The Virgin Mary is asking us to pray her Rosary more faithfully and passionately, by contemplating the joyful

[78] Letter to Annita, July 15, 1913.

mysteries and the mysteries of the Passion and glory of her Son. He wanted to associate it with the mystery of the Redemption, which saves us.... When you are saying your Rosary, the angels and saints join you. This is why I insist that you pray it with a deep contemplation and faith, while meditating on its mysteries with religious devotion. Pray it privately or in community, at home or outside, in church or on the street, with a simple heart, while following the way of the Virgin Mary, step by step, with her Son. Always pray it with a strong faith, for the unborn, those who suffer, work, and are dying. Pray it in unison with all of the righteous of the earth and all Marian communities. But pray it, above all, with the simplicity of little children, whose voice is united to the angels' voices. The world has never before needed your Rosary as much as today.

Prayers to Angels

There are many prayers we can say to thank the angels who watch over us. The best-known one is the novena to St. Michael the Archangel.[79]

Another very ancient prayer is the litany to the holy guardian angels, in which we pray, "Holy angels, who carry our prayers before God's throne, *pray for us.*"

The "angelic crown," or St. Michael Rosary, emerged from a revelation from St. Michael to a Portuguese Carmelite named Sr. Antónia d'Astónaco. The apparition was not officially recognized by the Church, but the devotion has been encouraged since 1851. St. Alphonsus Liguori believed that "St. Michael, greatly desiring

---

[79] It is offered online each year via the website Hozana.org.

the salvation of his devout servants, will not allow a person who maintains devotion to him to fall into God's displeasure. He will give him the strength to resist Hell's attacks. When St. Michael commends a soul to God, he obtains eternal salvation for him."

We celebrate angels on many occasions in the liturgical year: on September 29, the feast of the Archangels Michael, Gabriel, and Raphael; on October 2, the feast of the Holy Guardian Angels; and in the Votive Mass of the Guardian Angels.

On Prayer to One's Guardian Angel

May your good guardian angel always watch over you and be your guide on the rough path of life. May he always keep you in the grace of Jesus and hold you up with his hands so that you do not hurt your foot against a stone. May he protect you under his wings from all the deceits of the world, the devil, and the flesh.

Have great devotion ... to this beneficent angel. How consoling it is to know that we have a spirit who, from the womb to the tomb, never leaves us for an instant, not even when we dare to sin. And this heavenly spirit guides and protects us like a friend, a brother.

But it is very consoling to know that this angel prays unceasingly for us and offers God all of our good actions, our thoughts, and our desires, if they are pure.

Oh! For goodness' sake, don't forget this invisible companion, ever present, ever disposed to listen to us and even more ready to console us. Oh, wonderful intimacy! Oh, blessed companionship! If only we could understand it! Keep him always before your mind's eye. Remember this angel's presence often, thank him, pray to him, always keep up a good relationship. Open yourself up to him and confide your suffering to him. Be always afraid of offending the purity of his gaze. Know this, and keep it well present in your mind. He is easily offended, very sensitive. Turn to him in moments of supreme anguish, and you will experience his beneficent help.

Never say that you are alone in the battle against your enemies; never say that you have no one to whom you can open your heart and confide. It would be a grave injustice to this heavenly messenger.[80]

Prayer

Holy angel, you adore the Eternal Father's face, as you always see it. Because His supreme goodness committed you to caring for my soul, rescue it always by His grace. Enlighten my soul in the darkness, console my soul in its pain, warm my soul in the cold, defend my soul in its temptations, and rule over my soul for the rest of my life. Deign to pray with me. Because my prayers are cold and languishing, set them on fire with your burning love, and carry them up to the throne of God to offer them to Him.

—St. Charles Borromeo

---

[80] St. Pio of Pietrelcina, letter to Annita, July 15, 1913.

11

The Encounter for Those Who Do Not Pray

I invite you to read this chapter while listening
to "Dona Nobis Pacem" (traditional canon).

It was the spring of 1916. Three little shepherds were playing
while watching over their sheep, not far from the village of
Fatima. The most important things for Lucia, who was nine,
and her cousins Francisco, who was barely eight, and Jacinta,
who was six, were playing, dancing, and singing. Sr. Lucia later
admitted in her memoirs that "we got the sheep to obey us by
giving them our snacks. Thus, once we arrived at the pasture,
we could play in peace, for they did not move away from us."
Oh, they prayed. They never started their day without reciting a
Rosary. But the little rascals had their own technique. They said
only the beginning of the prayers on the beads: "Our Father," and
then "Hail, Mary," without going any further. It was better than
nothing. They had fun with the echoes: "One of their favorite
hobbies was to go into the hills, sit on a high rock, and say names
out loud. The name that resonated the best was Mary's."

When they did not go into the hills, they met near the well of
Lucia's parents. Jacinta shed big tears here when her cousin told
her about Jesus' Passion. Francisco and Jacinta had not yet gone

to their catechism class because the church was too far away. So Lucia, who had made her First Communion, explained to them what she had learned. That day, while they were playing, a strong wind shook the trees. The children looked up.

"What is happening—a storm?" Yet the weather was so nice!

"Oh, look, over there, above the trees! That light that is so white—it looks like snow."

The light approached them. They saw that this light was shaped like a very handsome fourteen- or fifteen-year-old young man. It was both transparent and dazzling, like a crystal that the sun rays passed through. Lucia recognized him since she had seen him a year earlier. He was with three little shepherdesses. (Her cousins Francisco and Jacinta, who were too young, were not yet allowed to join her). He seemed like "a statue of snow. The sun rays made it look a little transparent."

He said: "Do not be afraid! I am the Angel of Peace. Pray with me!"

The angel knelt down on the ground, bowed his head, and repeated this prayer three times: "My God, I believe, I adore, I hope, and I love Thee! I beg pardon for those who do not believe, do not adore, do not hope, and do not love Thee. Amen."

The children were initially struck by this encounter. They very often thought about it again and prayed as the angel had asked them to do. Then, little by little, they relaxed. They still prayed, but they also spent a lot of time playing. During the summer, while they were having fun near the well of Lucia's parents, the angel appeared to them for the second time:

"What are you doing? Pray! Pray a great deal! Bring peace to your homeland."

He introduced himself: "I am your guardian angel, Portugal's angel."

The angel visited them a third time while they were reciting the prayer that he had taught them. He was holding a chalice with a host was suspended over it. He gave the host to Lucia, who had already made her First Communion and shared the chalice between Francisco and Jacinta, who had not yet made theirs.

"Console your God," he said.

The three children continued to bow down and prayed for such a long time that, when they got up, they noticed that it was already dark and they had to go back home.

When the angel visited them for the third time, at the end of the summer or in the fall, they were enthusiastically praying on their knees, with their faces to the ground. The three children tirelessly repeated the prayer he had taught them.[81]

Bearing Witness to Our Faith

We know many people who do not believe in, adore, hope in, or love God. They are in our workplaces, neighborhoods, sports clubs, and even our families.

A century or two ago, each family included a rebellious uncle, who was a freethinker, and a headstrong person who scandalized others as much as he amused them by his iconoclastic words. Today, with a few exceptions, practicing Catholics are the ones who look like extraterrestrials or eccentrics in their families. But what has happened to the fervor of our prayer for unbelievers? There was always a little Thérèse or a little Anne who prayed for the rebellious uncle. There was the grandmother who recited her Rosary with ivory beads for the whole family. Do we no longer pray for those who live without God because there are too many of them?

---

[81] According to Sister Lucia's writings, *Memoirs of Sister Lucia* (Fatima, Portugal: Secretariado dos Pastorinhos, 2008).

Encounters with Angels

"What are you doing?" our stunned angels ask us. We find a trustworthy babysitter or a good sports club by word of mouth. Likewise, we touch hearts by the witness of our lives and our faith.

Jesus, of course, warned us that it would not be easy. "A prophet is not without honor, except in his own country" (Mark 6:4). But Jesus is counting on us. "Woe to me if I do not preach the gospel!" St. Paul cried out (1 Cor. 9:16). On the other hand, may we be happy if we share this treasure that we have received without deserving it!

In Notre-Dame-du-Laus, Benoîte Rencurel, the sanctuary's guardian, received from her angel this advice about welcoming visitors: "Speak gently with visitors, especially those who are far away from religion, and not harshly, for they would not benefit from these words." He also recommended that she not talk about this and that but only about God's love and salvation.

During the Second World War, Mother Yvonne-Aimée of Malestroit bore witness to her faith through acts of resistance, to such an extent that General de Gaulle decorated her with the Legion of Honor. She also got the Cross of War and the Resistance medal. She received parachutists, helped Jewish families, and hid and cared for wounded resistance fighters. On February 16, 1943, the Gestapo arrested her and took her to the Cherche-Midi prison. One of her spiritual sons, Fr. Paul Labutte, was waiting for her in her office. He was terribly anxious and was trying very hard to recite his Rosary. A noise made him jump. He saw Mother Yvonne-Aimée in the middle of the room. She looked around with great surprise:

"But ... this is my office!" she exclaimed and then sat down, exhausted and disheveled, in a chair. "I understand: my good angel freed me and brought me back here. He seized me in the prison yard, right when we were being put in a group to leave for

Germany. He took advantage of the hubbub and disorder, the darkness and the blackout that were created during the roundup."[82]

> *Oh! Be my hope,*
> *Angel of Paradise.*
> *When, on the narrow road*
> *That leads man to what is good,*
> *My foot gets tired or I doubt,*
> *Quickly stretch your hand out to me!*[83]

Let Us Become Saints

During the Visitation, the Virgin Mary was the model of evangelization. Because she was carrying Jesus in her body, she was at once the tabernacle containing the hidden Jesus;, the monstrance, with Jesus revealed to the world; and the pyx, with Jesus who is given to our brothers. Fr. Julián Carrón, who leads the Communion and Liberation movement, thinks that the beauty and strength of the Christian message are attractive:

> If it were deprived of its ability to bring out the world's beauty, Christianity would be reduced to an ethic and a discourse that would be unable to attract and take hold of man's heart.... Today, man expects the experience of an encounter with people for whom Christ is such a reality that their own lives have changed.[84]

---

[82] Fr. Paul Labutte, *Yvonne-Aimée de Jésus, "ma mère selon l'Esprit"* [Yvonne-Aimée of Jesus: "my mother according to the Spirit] (Paris: F.-X. de Guibert, 1997).

[83] H. Gauthier's prayer.

[84] "La vie des chrétiens fascine-t-elle encore?" [Are Christians' lives still fascinating?] *Famille chrétienne*, no. 2171, August 24–30, 2019, 10–11.

Encounters with Angels

There is only one way of transmitting the Gospel—by becoming saints! This is not politics: do what I say, not what I do. For our faith must be seen before being heard! We are to show an example, by leaning on the very strength of God, who reveals Himself through our weakness. Sr. Lucia, who was Our Lady of Fatima's messenger for almost ninety years, talked in her memoirs about her First Communion, which she was able to make when she was six (rather than ten, as was the custom). She could do this because she knew the catechism inside out:

> My mother gave me her final advice. She told me what she wanted me to say to our Lord when I received Him in my heart, and she left me with these words: "Above all, ask our Lord to make you a saint!" These words were indelibly etched in my heart. They were the first ones that I said to our Lord as soon as I received Him. Today, I still think I hear the echo of the voice of my mother repeating them to me.[85]

St. Augustine told us that we love what we know and we try to know what we love. A good evangelist is, first of all, a person of prayer, someone who knows how to feed on and rejoice in God's presence. Edith Stein, whose religious name was St. Teresa Benedicta of the Cross, was a Carmelite and a philosopher. She believed that angels support us in this task:

> The angels protect the locked sanctuary with reverent awe. They desire only to bring the soul there in order for her to surrender it to God.[86]

[85] Second Memoir, par. 5.
[86] Edith Stein [Teresa Benedicta of the Cross], *The Science of the Cross*, vol. 6 of *The Collected Works of Edith Stein*, trans.

Earthen Vessels

The paradox of the Christian life is that God expects everything from us—except perfection! Holiness, yes. Faultlessness, no. For would He have sent His beloved Son to His death on the Cross if we could become perfect through our own efforts and will? "We have this treasure in earthen vessels" (2 Cor. 4:7). This is what God loves in us. As the poet Charles Péguy confided to a friend:

I have an incredible guardian angel. He is even smarter than I am, my friend! I cannot escape his watching over me. Three times, I felt him grab me, tear me away from my wishes—from meditated, prepared, and desired actions. He has incredible devices!

We will be his witnesses, despite our sins, weaknesses, and limitations. Our guardian angels know us well. They help us become evangelists who want to lead others toward the mercy that they themselves have received:

I will be your best friend. I will be the one who knows everything about you. I will never judge you, for I understand your mistakes. I will never condemn you.[87]

We feel our weakness when going toward others who are weak and sinful, as we are. They are without pride or bravado and are filled with respect and zeal.

One day, while crossing the playground with other teachers, St. Bénilde (a member of the Congregation of the Brothers of the Christian Schools) remarked that one of them had not greeted

---

Josephine Koeppel, O.C.D. (Washington, DC: ICS Publications, 2002), chap. 13.

[87] St. John Mary Vianney, the Curé of Ars.

the schoolchildren. "Lift up your hat," he said. "Think about it: these children have guardian angels that you must pay tribute to."

Prayer

My oldest friend, mine from the hour
When first I drew my breath;
My faithful friend that shall be mine,
Unfailing, till my death.

Thou has been ever at my side.
My Maker to thy trust
Consigned my soul what time He framed
The infant child of dust.

And mine, O Brother of my soul,
When my release shall come;
Thy gentle arms shall lift me then,
Thy wings shall waft me home.[88]

---

[88] John Henry Newman, prayer to his guardian angel, "My oldest friend," the Oratory, 1853.

12

The Encounter at the End of the Day

I invite you to read this chapter while
listening to the most famous Sabbath
song, the "Lecha Dodi."

The men slowly and solemnly entered the synagogue, as if they
were clothed with the dignity of the king's sons. Meanwhile,
just before sunset, in a house that smelled of warm bread, in
front of the women and the young children, the hostess lit two
candles (one for "Remember" and one for "Observe"). She also
sang the blessing of the light. She meditated on the mystery of
the woman for a few seconds by turning her hands around the
flame three times and then bringing them back toward herself
as if to cover herself with its light. Just as darkness entered the
world through Eve, the light would come back into the world
through a woman.

The men left the synagogue. To honor the angels who accompanied them to the house, they sang the "Shalom Aleichem." A
Jewish commentary also says that these angels, when they arrived
at the house, would verify the good behavior and the observance
of the dictates there and report them to God. The report would
indicate whether the house was clean and the candles lit, the

breads of the *shabbat* or *hallot* prepared and covered on the table, and the meal ready. The liturgy would continue in the family. Ordinary life would be suspended until the following night. The blessed *shabbat* day was spreading its peace in people's hearts.

A Day Dedicated to the Lord

Rest is a biblical notion that we find starting with chapter 2 in Genesis: "God rested [on the seventh day] from all his work which he had done in creation." Jewish and Christian traditions made this a commandment.

Among the Ten Commandments that God gave Moses, the first two are about God Himself. The other seven concern the relationships of people among themselves. The third commandment, which is about resting in God, intersects the first two, like a link between divinity and humanity:

> Observe the sabbath day, to keep it holy, as the Lord your God commanded you. Six days you shall labor, and do all your work; but the seventh day is a sabbath to the Lord your God; in it you shall not do any work, you, or your son, or your daughter, or your manservant, or your maidservant, or your ox, or your ass, or any of your cattle, or the sojourner who is within your gates, that your manservant and your maidservant may rest as well as you. You shall remember that you were a servant in the land of Egypt, and the Lord your God brought you out thence with a mighty hand and an outstretched arm; therefore the Lord your God commanded you to keep the sabbath day. (Deut. 5:12–15)

We were lucky, during the four years that we spent in Libreville in Gabon, to visit a very small Jewish community, who willingly welcomed us for the great Seder feast, which is the first Jewish Passover meal. We knew most of the songs and hosted the evening. It is very enriching for us Christians to discover Judaism, the religion that Jesus chose to be born into. We understand Holy Thursday better by seeing the Seder being celebrated, and Pentecost by discovering Shavuot, and the Transfiguration thanks to the feast of Tabernacles, which is also called Sukkoth.

Thanks to Pope Benedict XVI, the Catholic Church improved the dialogue with our elder brothers. A letter from the Vatican Congregation for Divine Worship asked, for example, that the word *Yahweh* be suppressed from the biblical texts. This is an unfortunate transcription of God's name; it is both erroneous (we do not know which vowels were used) and disrespectful to the Jewish people. In fact, the sacred tetragram YHWH (*yod, heh, vav, heh*), which is the name of God that was revealed to Moses, was pronounced only by the high priest in the Temple once a year. With the destruction of the second Temple, it was impossible to carry out this practice, and the sacred name was no longer used until Jesus came to teach us the new name: *Abba*, Father, our Father.

Why not do the same thing for the *shabbat* or *Chabad?* The *shabbat* starts on Friday night,[89] eighteen minutes before sunset, or when the light is too dim to differentiate black from white. It ends on Saturday night. During this time, all work, long trips, and most human activities are forbidden, so that man can recognize himself as a creature and turns toward His Creator: "If you want

---

[89] In Judaism, as in Christianity, with the celebration of the festive vigils, the day starts the night before, for Genesis says: "There was evening and there was morning, one day" (Gen. 1:5).

the concept of God as Creator to come alive, you have to stop creating."[90]

God takes a break from the work of creation and contemplates it by decreeing that it is "very good"; the *shabbat* invites us likewise to contemplate God's works in our lives and to rejoice in them. We go from what passes to what lasts and from what is unfinished to what is accomplished:

On the day of the *shabbat*, the world is finished, and man is fulfilled. The *shabbat* is the daily reminder of this accomplishment.... The *shabbat* is there to remind us of what we want to be: to fulfill ourselves, to work on our personalities, to become aware of our unique character, and to acquire a sense of achievement.[91]

Stopping at the end of the week to celebrate and give thanks is to rediscover the meaning of transcendence and to recognize that we are dependent on a master craftsman, on love, and on a father:

We also try, during the day of the *shabbat*, to put God's presence into this world. We abstain from all creating, with the goal of reaffirming that we are not masters of our fate. Someone else is taking care of it.[92]

Jesus observed the *shabbat*, even if He provoked those who forgot its original meaning: "The sabbath was made for man, not man for the sabbath" (Mark 2:27). He even respected it in

---

[90] Mrs. Lori Palatnik, "Les règles du *Chabbat* pour les débutants" [Sabbath rules for beginners], Aish.fr, https://www.aish.fr/print/?contentID=134031083.
[91] Ibid.
[92] Ibid.

His death since He stayed in the tomb on Holy Saturday and rested from the work of redemption (and not of creation) that He accomplished.

Sunday's Meaning

Christians believe that Sunday is Resurrection Day. It is the first day of the week and the eighth day of the world to come. The word *Sunday* comes from the Latin *dies Domini* or *dies dominica*, "the Lord's Day." The first Christians, who were of Jewish descent, continued to celebrate both the *shabbat* and Sunday for three centuries. Then Sunday, the day when the Eucharist was celebrated, took precedence over the *shabbat*. We can imagine that it was difficult for this era's social life to have two consecutive days of rest. St. John Paul II told us that "we move from the 'Sabbath' to the 'first day after the Sabbath', from the seventh day to the first day: the *dies Domini* becomes the *dies Christi!*"[93] Whereas, the *shabbat* commemorates the Creation, Sunday reminds us of the new creation that Jesus obtained for us: "In effect, Sunday is the day above all other days which summons Christians to remember the salvation that was given to them in baptism and which has made them new in Christ."[94]

Individual prayer is very important in the Christian religion. But, in order to sanctify Sunday, we are invited to "stick together." We are encouraged to gather together (this is the first meaning of the word *Church*) and to meet one another in order for fraternal communities to emerge in our cities and neighborhoods. "It is important therefore that they come together to

---

[93] John Paul II, apostolic letter *Dies Domini*, on keeping the Lord's Day holy (May 31, 1998), no. 18.

[94] Ibid., no. 25.

express fully the very identity of the Church, the *ekklesia*, the assembly called together by the risen Lord."[95] Thus, each local church is the image of the people of God. This includes men and women, children, those who are engaged, the young, the elderly, priests and deacons, committed laypeople, parish team members, liturgical team participants, choir members, and musicians ... They all participate in the beauty and radiance of the celebration.

Before the French Revolution and during the confraternities that governed each profession, it was stipulated that, in the case of the goldsmiths who had worked on a Sunday or public holiday, the money that was collected on these occasions would be used to offer a large dinner for the poor in the Hôtel-Dieu (the hospice) on Easter Sunday.

Sunday's Joy

This day that the Lord made is a joyful feast day! Whereas the *shabbat* is marked by the nostalgia of waiting, joy characterizes Sunday: the joy of Jesus' Resurrection, "the first-born from the dead" (Col. 1:18), the joy of the promise of our own resurrection, the joy of the universe that is finally reconciled: "Blessed is the one who raised the great day of Sunday above all days. Heaven and earth, and angels and men, abandon themselves to joy."[96]

Sunday rest was not always granted by civil societies. Then it became an entitlement in our Western societies. The drift toward the "weekend" now takes away part of its meaning, and the holiday has become a day of leisure at all costs:

---

[95] Ibid., no. 31.
[96] Marionite hymn of the Church of Antioch.

Unfortunately, when Sunday loses its fundamental meaning and becomes merely part of a "weekend", it can happen that people stay locked in a horizon so limited that they can no longer see the "heavens". Hence, though ready to celebrate, they are really incapable of doing so.[97]

Sunday is a day of being open to others, of fraternity and peace, and a day to spend with family. During this time, we can care about the people in our community who are alone or fragile. What family would be generous enough to reach out to the single mother who is having a hard time managing her young children, or the elderly lady in the house next door who never has visitors, or the sour uncle whom nobody invites over anymore?

As a day of prayer, communion and joy, Sunday resounds throughout society, emanating vital energies and reasons for hope. Sunday is the proclamation that time, in which he who is the Risen Lord of history makes his home, is not the grave of our illusions, but the cradle of an ever new future, an opportunity given to us to turn the fleeting moments of this life into seeds of eternity.[98]

Let us make Sunday a real feast for our children. May it not be a day in which we hang out in old jogging suits in front of the television. But let it be the incarnated witness of our faith in Jesus' Resurrection. Here are some practical ideas to make this day unlike the others:

• *Prepare for Mass.* Our children will not experience the Mass as a chore that interrupts their games if we take the

[97] John Paul II, *Dies Domini*, no. 4.
[98] Ibid., no. 84.

time to prepare for it with them. We can do this by reading the Gospel of the day, by providing coloring pages that are connected with this Gospel, and by explaining a specific point about the celebration. I recall a Mass that was reverently experienced by our five children because, right beforehand, we had talked to them about Padre Pio, who saw angels around the altar during the elevation of the Host.

• *Plan a good meal and decorate the table.* The children will be glad to add their inventive touch to it. The father or the oldest children can make dinner or pick up pizza so that the mother can breathe a little.

• *Offer a family activity.* Even if teens have homework or parents need to do some gardening, administrative work, or overdue ironing, it is important to reserve an hour or two for an activity that unites the family, whether it be a hike, a visit, or a board game. A film that everyone watches together is fun, but it should be reserved for the evening because it hinders communication and the discovery of each person's hidden talents.

• *Have a family conversation.* Nothing strengthens a family more than listening to one another. It can be a round-table discussion during the meal, when everyone talks about his best time of the week, for example. Such conversation also provides an opportunity to confide problems, concerns, or heartaches. Parents can share worries they are bearing. But be careful. This is not about loading crushing burdens on the children. It can, however, help them to understand that they too quickly blame themselves for certain ill-tempered reactions or silences on the part of their parents. What is communicated seems less heavy, and good ideas can come to mind. Above all, where two or three are gathered in His name, Jesus is there among them (see Matt. 18:20). He manifests His presence and offers His consolation.

• *Pray together.* At the end of this day on which all the family members have been able to recharge their batteries spiritually and emotionally, set aside time to entrust the week to God.

There is no ready-made recipe, for Sunday is to be renewed over and over again — when the children are little, when they become teens, when they have left the house, and so forth. May Jesus, who is "the Lord of the Sabbath," be our Sunday host so that we may experience it as a foretaste of a happy eternity, when we will contemplate Him on a day without a sunset: "We need this encounter which brings us together, which gives us space for freedom, which lets us see beyond the bustle of everyday life to God's creative love, from which we come and towards which we are travelling."[99]

Meditation

And while they were gazing into heaven as he went, behold, two men stood by them in white robes, and said, "Men of Galilee, why do you stand looking into heaven? This Jesus, who was taken up from you into heaven, will come in the same way as you saw him go into heaven." Then they returned to Jerusalem from the mount called Olivet, which is near Jerusalem, a sabbath day's journey away. (Acts 1:10–12)

[99] Benedict XVI, homily, September 9, 2007, Vienna.

Encounters with Angels

Shalom Aleichem

Shalom aleichem, malachei ha-shareit,
malachei elyon,
mi-melech malchei ha-mlachim,
Ha-Kadosh Baruch Hu.

Peace be upon you, ministering angels,
messengers of the Most High God,
Messengers of the King of Kings of Kings,[100]
the Holy One, blessed be He.

Bless me with peace, messengers of peace,
messengers of the Most High God,
Messengers of the King of Kings,
the Holy One, blessed be He.

Go in peace, messengers of peace,
messengers of the Most High God,
Messengers of the King of Kings,
the Holy One, blessed be He.[101]

[100] Emphatic form: the very, very great King.
[101] Song on the eve of the *shabbat*, at the end of the seventeenth
century.

13

The Encounter in the Middle of the Night

I invite you to read to this chapter while
listening to Pergolesi's *Stabat Mater*.

Jesus knew about serene nights when coolness and silence re-
placed the day's activity and heat. These were nights that invited
the body to rest. They seemed to touch the earth, and God's
presence was very close. Jesus was so happy to taste the joy of
this rediscovered heart-to-heart talk that He spent these nights
praying. He had to learn about nights that were full of anxiety,
remorse, and fear. These were nights that grabbed you by the
throat and gripped you like a vice. They were nights of suffering
whose hours were drawn out and condensed into a single fear.
Would daylight return? He had to learn the desperate loneliness of someone who had no more love or confidence and the
constant bitterness of the one who had messed everything up
and lost everything.

The cup of the New Covenant stayed in the house after everyone had drunk from it. The cup that was presented to Him
overflowed with bitterness, crimes, rape, betrayals, lies, cowardice,
hatred, and the blasphemy of humanity, yesterday, today, and
tomorrow.

Encounters with Angels

"My Father, if it be possible, let this cup pass from me; nevertheless, not as I will, but as thou wilt" (Matt. 26:39). "I will drink this cup to join your rebellious and lost children up to this point. I will drink it so that nobody among them will know the despair of the trial that one goes through by himself."

In this instant, when He was perfectly free—free as nobody had ever been so far—the true God who could separate Himself from the true God—in this tiny second when everything could tilt between "my will" and "Yours," all of Creation's fate was at stake. But there was no hesitation in His heart, which was turned toward God's silence. His freedom was that of love, and His will was that of the Father. He gave Himself as He had given everything—His heart since He came into the world, His spirit in this night of agony, and, finally, His body when dawn would break.

Then the angel came to comfort Him. The three apostles, His three witnesses, could not keep watch. Their eyes were weighed down with sleep, and they did not understand what He was asking of them. But the angel kept watch: the luminous angel who brightened the darkness, the pure angel who kept crimes away, the confident angel who pushed away doubts. The angel brought all of God's tenderness with him and received this yes—I want it—Yours, Yours.

The anguish that arose was so strong that Jesus' sweat became like drops of blood that fell on the ground. It was the ground that gratefully collected them while the men were sleeping. "His blood be on us and on our children" (Matt. 27:25); "Father, forgive them; for they do not know what they are saying; for they do not know what they are doing" (see Luke 23:34). "It is for this reason that I have come to this hour—the hour of diving into the waters of death in order to get you out of them."

Some lights were piercing the night. It was not yet dawn. They were torches of the troop that came to arrest Him and put Him to death.

The hour of darkness went by. This was God's hour. Jesus said to them: "It is I."[102]

Throughout the Night

In the darkest part of the night, when anxiety seems to rule over the world and hope has deserted it, and there are no more strong men or heroes, we all become children. The night is a refuge for the one who peacefully falls asleep, with a sense of accomplishment. It seems endless for the sick person who is suffering, the anxious person who tosses and turns a hundred times, the insomniac who cannot escape his repetitive thoughts, the abused child whom the night has betrayed, the battered woman who stays awake because of her pain, the prisoner who is more confined by the night, the poor person who does not dare to close his eyes for fear that the little that he has will be stolen, or the dying person who will no longer see daybreak.

Jesus has joined us in the deep agony of dark nights. Before the Good Friday offering and before the Passion and the loud cry on the Cross that snatched humanity from death, there was this night of abandonment when His sweat became like drops of blood. "Hematidrosis is a condition in which capillary blood vessels that feed the sweat glands rupture, causing them to exude blood, occurring under conditions of extreme physical or emotional stress."[103]

---

[102] See this account in Matthew 26:36-44, Mark 14:32-40, and Luke 22-39-46.

[103] "Hematidrosis," *Wikipedia*, last edited May 5, 2021, https://en.wikipedia.org/wiki/Hematidrosis.

Encounters with Angels

Jesus spent His nights in prayer. But in the Garden of the Winepress, where He was pressed like a piece of fruit from which blood flows, His freedom met our anxieties and fears. The night is dark for the one who is tortured by regrets. It is long for the one who suffers. The night is gentle for the one who rests in God:

> By day the LORD commands his steadfast love,
> and at night his song is with me,
> a prayer to the God of my life. (Ps. 42:8)

> *De noche iremos, de noche,*
> *que para encontrar la fuente*
> *solo la sed nos alumbra,*
> *solo la sed nos alumbra.*

> At night, we will go find the source.
> Thirst is the only thing that illuminates us.[104]

The Little World of the Night

A young woman who works in food service returns home in the middle of the night and meets some drunk partygoers who call out to her as if she were a drinking companion. "Not everyone on the street at night has come out of a nightclub," she replies, annoyed.

Let us think about this. There are three million of them in France — all those who work at night in the service of others in the health field: emergency doctors, on-call doctors, the nursing staff in hospitals, maternity wards, and retirement homes. There are those who work in transportation and delivery jobs, in food service and hotel work, in auditoriums, concert halls, and movie

---

[104] Jacques Berthier, Taizé song.

136

theaters, and in factories whose production is continuous. There are those who clean when everyone has left, soldiers, police officers, and security guards, the little grocer on the streetcorner, and the baker who gets up to prepare his dough so that we can have fresh bread when we wake up.

They go to bed when the city wakes up. They try to sleep despite the noise, the unrest, the ring of the doorbell, the horn blasts, and the light.

Prayer

Watch, O Lord, with those who wake, or watch, or weep tonight, and give Your angels and saints charge over those who sleep.

Tend Your sick ones, O Lord Christ.

Rest Your weary ones.

Bless Your dying ones.

Soothe Your suffering ones.

Pity Your afflicted ones.

Shield Your joyous ones, and all for Your love's sake.

Amen.[105]

We all know people who suffer from severe insomnia, which is the illness of our century, when everything moves too fast. At night, the anxieties and questions that we have managed to hide in the activities of our busy days surface. If we can, let us apply the advice of the English poet William Blake: "Think in the morning. Act in the noon. Eat in the evening. Sleep in the night."

"I think of thee upon my bed, and meditate on thee in the watches of the night; for thou hast been my help, and in the

---

[105] Traditional prayer attributed to St. Augustine.

shadow of thy wings I sing for joy" (Ps. 63:6–7). What are God's wings? They are the angel's wings, the friendly presence at night.

Prayer

O most holy angel of God, appointed by God to be my guardian, I give you thanks for all the benefits you have bestowed on my body and soul. I praise and glorify you that you condescend to assist me with such patient fidelity and to defend me against all the assaults of my enemies. Blessed be the hour in which you were assigned to be my guardian, defender, and patron. Blessed be your love and all your care. You do not cease to hasten my salvation! I ask you to forgive me for having so often resisted your suggestions, which sadden you, my good friend. I resolve to obey you in the future and to serve God faithfully.[106]

Morning Prayer to My Guardian Angel

Good morning, my guardian angel. I love you tenderly. You looked after me tonight while I was sleeping. Please protect me on this day from harm, accidents, and offending God, at least mortally. Amen.

Evening Prayer to My Guardian Angel

Good evening, my guardian angel, I thank you for having looked after me on this day. Offer all my heartbeats to God while I sleep. Amen.

—St. John Mary Vianney, the Curé of Ars

---

[106] St. Gertrude of Helfta.

Part 3

Angels, Our Fellow Travelers

For he will give his angels charge of you
to guard you in all your ways.
On their hands they will bear you up,
lest you dash your foot against a stone.

—Psalm 91:11–12

The third mission of the angels, because they are faithful
and loving, is to aid us. They guide and protect us and
watch over us. They defend us from danger, strengthen us
when we are discouraged, and console us in our trials.

14

The Loving Encounter

I invite you to read this chapter while listening to
Berlioz's *Romeo and Juliet* (act 2). This symphony
is not as well known as Prokoviev's ballet of the
same name, but I find it to be very moving.

Once upon a time, there was an unhappy man whose father had
become blind.

Once upon a time, there was an unhappy young girl who did
not find a husband.

Once upon a time, there was an angel who was sent by God
to unite two families that were in need and help them to be
happy again.

In this episode from the book of Tobit (chapters 3–12), we
meet the archangel Raphael, whose name means "God heals."
In two places, Nineveh and Ecbatana, Tobit and Sarah were
simultaneously praying desperately to God. They would rather
die than bear the situations they were in! Tobit had become
blind, and Sarah was being harassed by a demon that killed the
seven men who had married her. "So Raphael was sent to heal
the two of them."

Encounters with Angels

Tobit wanted to retrieve, before he died, a sum of money that was deposited at a friend's home in Rages in Media. He decided to send his son Tobiah, who sought a companion for the trip. "He found Raphael, who was an angel, but Tobiah did not know it."

"Can you go with me to Rages in Media?" Tobiah asked him. "Are you acquainted with that region?"

"I will go with you; I am familiar with the way."

The angel, who called himself Azariah, took the road with the young Tobiah. To comfort his wife, who was anxiously crying, Tobit said to her: "Do not worry ... for a good angel will go with him; his journey will be successful, and he will come back safe and sound."

On the second night, while they were near Ecbatana, Raphael announced that they would stop at the home of a man who was related to Tobit. His daughter was destined for him. But the young man had heard of her strange curse: "I am afraid, for it is not she whom the demon attacks but anyone who approaches her."

Raphael gave him a remedy: "You will save her." He praised her. "She is a wise, courageous, and very beautiful girl." It did not take long for Tobiah to be convinced. "He fell in love with her and yearned deeply for her."

The young man did everything that Raphael had advised him to do. He married Sarah and managed to drive the demon away. Before being united, Tobiah and Sarah recited a beautiful prayer that many couples have used over the centuries. Tobiah celebrated his wedding for fourteen days and, with absolute confidence, let Raphael go to Rages by himself to retrieve his father's money.

Then Raphael and Tobiah returned to Nineveh to inform the elderly Tobit, who thought that his son was dead. Following Raphael's directions, Tobiah healed his father of his blindness.

When the two immensely grateful men wanted to thank the
angel by giving him half of the riches they had brought back from
the trip, Raphael took them aside and revealed the truth to them:

Praise God and give thanks to him; exalt him and give
thanks to him in the presence of all the living for what
he has done for you.... God sent me to heal you and your
daughter-in-law Sarah. I am Raphael, one of the seven
holy angels who present the prayers of the saints and
enter into the presence of the glory of the Holy One....
When I was with you, I was not acting out of any favor
on my part, but by God's will.... Even though you saw me
eat and drink, I did not eat or drink anything; what you
were seeing was a vision. So now bless the Lord on earth
and give thanks to God. Look, I am ascending to the one
who sent me.

They were deeply moved and happy, and that is what they did:
"So they confessed the great and wonderful works of God, and
acknowledged that the angel of the Lord had appeared to them."

The Third Dimension of Marriage

You may know the kind of TV show that involves matchmaking,
such as *Married at First Sight*. It starts a little like the book of Tobit:

Once upon a time, there was an unhappy young man whose
love affairs had ended badly.

Once upon a time, there was an unhappy young girl who did
not find a husband.

Once upon a time, a team of scientists decided to bring them
together because of the number of things they had in common.

This is where everything gets out of hand to give us a sad picture
of couples who have forgotten—who have not even known—the

third dimension of their marriage. The guest of honor, God Himself, is not there. The one who invented and blessed the marriage is not present in these stories that have merely a human point of view in which people separate after having admitting that they have failed. This reinforces a sense of self-denigration and a lack of self-confidence in these unhappy candidates.

Yet marriage is a gift from God that is incredibly beautiful and unexpectedly powerful. It is so far above the pale images that are seen on TV shows, which focus on the choice of dress or the planning of the reception. A Jewish joke says: "What has God done since He completed creation? He does weddings!"

A Very Important Sacrament

The Sacrament of Marriage that engaged couples share in the presence of a priest or deacon is powerfully effective:

> For God Himself is the author of matrimony, endowed as it is with various benefits and purposes (cf. Gen. 1:26, Wisd. 2:23). All of these have a very decisive bearing on the continuation of the human race, on the personal development and eternal destiny of the individual members of a family, and on the dignity, stability, peace and prosperity of the family itself and of human society as a whole.[107]

We can see a beautiful flow of love that resembles the Holy Trinity in the complementary nature of different states of life. Children are born from the love of a man and woman that is

---

[107] Second Vatican Council, Pastoral Constitution on the Church in the Modern World *Gaudium et Spes* (December 7, 1965), no. 48.

blessed by God. Vocations to the priesthood and religious life emerge in this fertile ground. In turn, the clergy help young people find their vocation and create holy Christian families.

Today, it is difficult to swim against the tide to bear witness to faithful and lasting marital love. Trust, forgiveness, dialogue, and common prayer—all that forms a union on solid foundations must be learned. This is even more the case today than in the past, for we have fewer and fewer examples of Christian couples before our eyes. Let us ask the angels, who are watching over our marriages, to make us stronger each day in the face of temptations and storms by helping us to keep in mind all the good that God has done for us.

"He Will Love You as He Loves Me"

It was a demon that "watched over" Sarah's virginity in the book of Tobit. It was the other way around in the golden legend of St. Cecilia, virgin and martyr, who died in Rome in 230. Even though she had taken a vow of virginity, her parents gave her in marriage to a pagan named Valerian. When the wedding night arrived, the young girl warned her husband that an angel was watching over her and her body's purity "with extreme care."[108]

"If he notices, in the least, that you are touching me and being impelled by a love that is contaminating me, he will strike you right away. You will lose the flower of your charming youth. But if he sees that you love me with a sincere love, he will love you as he loves me, and he will show you his glory."

"If you want me to believe you," Valerian answered, "make me see this angel. If I make sure that he is really an angel of God, I

---

[108] See this passage about St. Cecilia's marriage in *The Golden Legend*, by Jacques de Voragine.

will do what you exhort me to do. But if you love another man, I will strike both of you with my sword."

"If you believe in the real God and receive a Christian Baptism, you will be able to see the angel who watches over me."

The young man accepted this and prepared for the Baptism that he would receive at Easter. When he looked at Cecilia, he then saw a luminous angel with dazzling wings near her. He converted his brother Tiburtius, and all three of them died as martyrs for their Christian Faith.

St. Cecilia's example must not make us think that the Church considers marital relationships bad. On the contrary, spouses who are united "become one flesh" (Gen. 2:24), thus becoming an image of God's love.

God is love and in himself he lives a mystery of personal loving communion. Creating the human race in his own image ... God inscribed in the humanity of man and woman the vocation, and thus the capacity and responsibility, of love and communion. (CCC 2331)

In the early days of their marriage, Louis and Zélie Martin abstained from sexual relations, thinking that their life as a couple would be holier as a result. They did this until a priest told them that God's plan of love for couples was that the man and woman are united even in their bodies.

As St. John Paul II reminded us in his Theology of the Body, by developing the Church's doctrine, the union of bodies extends the union of hearts.

The acts in marriage by which the intimate and chaste union of the spouses takes place are noble and honorable;

the truly human performance of these acts fosters the self-giving they signify and enriches the spouses in joy and gratitude (GS 49 § 2). (CCC 2362)

At this time, when sexual relationships are evaluated according to their performances and the degree of enjoyment that is achieved, believers have a testimony to offer—first, through fidelity, then through the respect and tenderness that presides over a marital union. Married couples who love each other in the sight of God respect the other, who is not a partner but a spouse—the one we are attached to in an indissoluble way—even in his modesty and reserve. The attention, sensitivity, humor, and joy of sharing do not remain at the foot of the bed with the clothes. They are an integral part of the marital act. One spouse does not have to impose practices on the other one that would be displeasing to that person. Each one maintains his freedom and dignity, as in all the other areas of their life as a couple.

Contrary to the ideas that are being disseminated, sexual harmony is not built in one night. It takes time. We must be won over. We have to discover each other. The body of my spouse is an unknown territory that I will explore throughout the years. I will be going from one discovery to another in an incessant renewal that makes light of routine.

This is a catch-22 situation. The loving gestures that are shared during the day, the small acts of kindness, smiles, and discussions nourish the physical union, which, in turn, illuminates our whole day with its tenderness and joyous bond. The more we love each other in an area of our life as a couple, the more we will love each other in the other ones, and the more we will look for opportunities to increase this love.

Encounters with Angels

1 + 1 = 3

Our whole life as a couple will be confronted with the challenge of finding the right distance and balance between separations and times together. We cannot be perpetually merged. That would be destructive, for both people need to nourish their personalities by engaging with the outside world. On the contrary, if we do not share anything, how do we find each other?

God put man and woman face-to-face. They do not absorb each other. They are both fully themselves when facing each other. This is why we become not one but three. Our relationship as a couple opens up to the world—to the presence of others, to the welcoming of children who are born out of our love, and to the blessing of God, who helps us rise a little more each day by relying on each other. As Bl. Charles de Habsbourg-Lorraine said to his fiancée, Zita, the day before their wedding: "Now we must mutually help each other get to Heaven."

Like the Angels

Getting to Heaven ...

What will happen after we die? Will all this love be lost? Jesus said these words, which can worry us: "When they rise from the dead, they neither marry nor are given in marriage, but are like angels in heaven" (Mark 12:25). Does that mean that spouses will ignore each other and be like strangers?

"Like angels": Do angels, who are always at our sides, ignore us? Aren't angels the witnesses of this privileged tradition that can exist in the sight of God?

Nothing that we have experienced will be lost. On the contrary, the love of spouses will shine with a thousand lights in that other life, where every loving gesture will be magnified. We will fully discover the wholeness that we have looked for—sometimes in suffering—because our communication will be perfect. We will know what we are feeling, what we have experienced, and what we want. There will be no more misunderstandings and false interpretations. We will meet in a perfect communion of minds and hearts.

We will be *like* the angels, but we will also be *with* the angels. They will continue to accompany us and guide us, as they do now. We will benefit more from their help and presence, for we will be freed from the sin that weighs us down in so many areas. Let us think of mistrust, suspicion, fear, jealousy, competitiveness, pride, the desire to dominate, the thirst for power, lust, the wish to seize what someone else possesses, and so forth. How free we will be without these chains that prevent us from fully enjoying the fraternal or marital relationship!

But bodies? There will no longer be a union of bodies because we will no longer need it. We will, like the angels, experience everything through our spirits, without having to go through the vehicle of the body. You may think, "I am going to miss that!" and remember particularly successful times when you felt that you were together as one being. But this will still be the case in Heaven! The privileged connection of spouses will last. It will be enhanced and sanctified. The connection to the body will simply be different, just as Jesus was neither very different nor completely the same after His Resurrection: "See my hands and my feet, that it is I myself; handle me, and see; for a spirit has not flesh and bones as you see that I have" (Luke 24:39).

We will say: "It is really you!" when we recognize our spouses. Heaven's secret is that our relationship will be perfect without being exclusive. Our love will be complete for itself and for others, for we will receive it directly from God our Father, whom we will see face-to-face. His gaze will fill all our desires to an overwhelming degree that we cannot even imagine. We will no longer desire anything because our entire being will be both desire and fullness.

Children of the Resurrection

This same passage from the Gospel, which was told by St. Luke this time, emphasizes the Resurrection: "Those who are accounted worthy to attain to that age and to the resurrection from the dead neither marry nor are given in marriage, for they cannot die any more, because they are equal to angels and are sons of God, being sons of the resurrection" (Luke 20:35–36).

"They cannot die." By leading us toward holiness and intimacy with God, marriage—like all sacraments—keeps death away from us. This is not a physical death, which is one of humanity's necessary passages, or dying to ourselves, by which we renounce the chains that bind us. Marriage takes us away from the death of the soul, which results from being separated from God. Jesus does not stop saying this throughout the Gospels—by becoming children of God, we receive true and eternal life. A part of us has received death as a legacy by growing older, by receiving wounds that pull us to the dark side, and by our limitations and destructive choices. Another part of us, the purest and unchanging part, is marked with life and love. This luminous part is established through the sacraments. It is reinforced through our personal prayer lives and grows each time we love our loved ones.

What better school of love is there than the family? Before even opening our eyes, starting with the maternal womb, we notice shouts or prayers, discord or harmony, rejection or desire. We begin the great apprenticeship of life in the family. This is why the family is a school of resurrection. There we learn that love is unconditionally spread, that forgiveness restores our lives, that prayer is the secret of peace of heart, and that we do not save ourselves.

Jesus often compared the Kingdom of God to a great banquet. Yet we will no longer be hungry or thirsty, we will no longer have any stomachaches, and we will no longer be tired. Why the resurrection of the body, in this case? As Jesus kept and showed us His glorious wounds, our bodies will keep the witness of love that we have received and given. This is why, in Heaven, we will be free in our bodies—like angels. But we will keep the traces of our earthly passage that will entail so many proofs of love.

We will only have one question when we cross Heaven's gate: Have I loved enough?

I have taken you in my arms, and I love you, and I prefer you to my life itself. For the present life is nothing, and my most ardent dream is to spend it with you in such a way that we may be assured of not being separated in the life reserved for us.[109]

This is the prayer that John Chrysostom recommended when he celebrated a wedding.

Prayer

Blessed art thou, O God of our fathers,
  and blessed be thy holy and glorious name for ever.
Let the heavens and all thy creatures bless thee.
Thou madest Adam and gavest him Eve his wife
  as a helper and support.
From them the race of mankind has sprung.

---

[109] St. John Chrysostom, *Hom. in Eph.* 20,8: PG 62,146–147, quoted in CCC 2365.

*Thou didst say, "It is not good that the man should be
    alone;*
*   let us make a helper for him like himself."*
And now, O Lord, I am not taking this sister of mine
because of lust, but with sincerity.
Grant that I may find mercy and may
grow old together with her. (Tobit 8:5–8)

15

The Angel on the Road

I invite you to read this chapter while listening to *Aimer
ou mourir—Chants d'amour au bien aimé* (To love or
die: songs of love to the beloved), performed by Sylvie
Buisset. The 2004 CD assembles ten poems of great
mystics such as St. John of the Cross, St. Teresa of
Ávila, St. Gertrude of Helfta, and Agnes of Langeac.

The book of Numbers introduces us to a strange and controversial
character named Balaam, a fortune-teller from the region of Moab
(see Numbers 22 and 23). Right after the episode with the bronze
serpent, Moses and his people, who were in exodus in the desert,
were going to meet Balaam. King Balak commanded him to curse
Israel in order to halt its progression, for this is how influential
Balaam was: "He whom you bless is blessed, and he whom you
curse is cursed." Balaam was living in Pethor in Mesopotamia
while he listened to the Word of God. This was a region where
people worshipped Belphegor (Baal Peor). Balaam let the king of
Moab shower him with gifts, which real prophets did not accept.

God authorized Balaam to leave with the king's messengers.
But Balaam disobeyed Him by leaving in a hurry. He rode on a
donkey behind Moab's princes. Suddenly, on the way, the donkey

found herself face-to-face with the angel of the Lord, who was ready to kill Balaam, with his sword in hand. The donkey turned away from the path three times in order to save her master. Balaam got angry each time, until the animal started talking on the third time:

"What have I done to you, that you have struck me these three times?"

"Because you have made sport of me. I wish I had a sword in my hand, for then I would kill you!"

At that moment, Balaam's eyes were opened, and he saw the angel of the Lord standing in the road in front of him. The angel was ready to strike him with his sword. Balaam immediately bowed down, falling on his face.

"And the angel of the LORD said to him, 'Why have you struck your ass these three times? Behold, I have come forth to withstand you, because your way is perverse before me.'"

Balaam offered to return home.

"Go with the men; but only the word which I bid you, that shall you speak."

Balaam ended up blessing the chosen people three times rather than cursing them. This angered King Balak.

The Path of Life

When I was growing up, my family often sang together. My father taught us a lot of songs. I later learned that they were scout songs. I cannot resist quoting some of the words that still come to mind while I'm hiking.

> It is good to march
> In the wind of France
> Under the sun

The Angel on the Road

By following the road
Under a summer sky,
March, life is calling you!
Hurl your joyous song toward the sky
Your route will be beautiful![110]

From *Vents frais* (Fresh wind), we learned to sing a canon, and we were first introduced to polyphony with *Ma chaumière* (My cottage). It was a joy to hear my children sing it in turn.

"Tomorrow, Starting with the Dawn"

Life is like a road. We take it one day at a time. Why do we say that the early bird catches the worm? It is perhaps because there is a purity or renewal in each dawn — as if every possibility were within easy reach. I love to run before breakfast. On some mornings, there is a feeling of conquest in nature when the prickly wind bends the wheat or the frost sparkles on the branches. Each bird song seems to include a promise and each flower a new hope.

Then the path rises and crosses others and bristles with pointed stones that wound us and brambles that hold us back. Jesus warned us. The path is not a long, straight line at the edge of a canal! The road and life make us suffer and cry. But the angels, our faithful fellow travelers, accompany us. They are near us in our joys and trials. Neither our indifference nor our ingratitude discourages them from offering their support and comfort. "I send an angel before you, to guard you on the way and to bring you to the place which I have prepared" (Exod. 23:20).

---

[110] Francine Cockenpot, "Dans le vent de France" [In the wind of France], on the album *Vents du Nord* (Winds of France) (1945).

Encounters with Angels

Nonetheless, if we gave them free rein, their field of action would really be enlarged! Our angel, like Benoîte Rencurel's angel, who removed the brambles from her path, could send us more signs of his presence. Our heart needs to be attentive to interpret these messages, but how accurate and pertinent they are!

Agnes of Langeac attended Mass in a church that was far from where she lived. If she came back late, her father beat her. So, when she left the church, she saw "a little lamb that was very gentle and beautiful" that brought her back home. Sometimes the angel was shaped like a white butterfly or a little bird.

I recall, when we were decorating our backpacks, that we recopied this quote from Jacques Higelin:

> To all those who stretched out their hand
> To my soul that was lost on the paths of doubt
> I send you friendship and deep respect
> From the angel with clenched fists that watches
> over my route.

Our road is winding, and it is rarely very clear where it is leading us. Sometimes the descent is rough, and everything seems to be going too fast. At times, the slope is so steep that we have to make decisions on the spot. A famous soccer coach has given us "Five tips for a winning mindset":[111]

1. *Eliminate negative thoughts*: "I can't do it, I'm not up to it, I fear ..." Do not hesitate or doubt. Commit yourself completely without questioning yourself.

---

[111] Arsène Wenger, "Cinq conseils pour avoir un mental de gagnant" [Five tips for a winning mindset]. The video is available on *Brut sport FR*, www.brut.media.

2. *Do not worry about what others think.* The truth is found within us. Others cannot live our lives for us.
3. *Never give up trying.* Set a goal for yourself, and do everything to attain it. Do not give up.
4. *Do not think too much.* Learn to master your fears by removing doubt and moving forward. Keep concentrating. Remain in the present moment.
5. *Draw energy from your defeats.* Failure is disappointing, and it hurts. But we must maintain an adult and mature attitude and not blame our failures on others or on external events. We have to be honest in evaluating ourselves and discerning what we were lacking and come back stronger by drawing energy from our failures.

We can conclude from this that talent without effort does not lead to anything. To paraphrase St. Francis of Assisi in the last words of his "Simple Prayer,"[112] we could say: "For it is in falling down that we get back up. It is in getting lost that we find our way again. It is after exhausting our strength that we rest. It is in forgetting ourselves that we find ourselves. It is when we are at peace with ourselves that we experience the most beautiful encounters."

The Right to Doubt

Doubt is not a sin in itself. We see that many saints first experienced a period of doubt before accepting their missions. Let us

---

[112] "For it is in giving that we receive; it is in pardoning that we are pardoned; and it is in dying that we are born to eternal life." This well-known prayer is usually attributed to St. Francis of Assisi. But it seems that it dates only from 1912.

recall the prophet Elijah, mentioned in chapter 3. He was ready to die, but an angel came to feed and help him. This crisis allowed Elijah to be confirmed in his mission.

Doubt lets us pass through a faith that we received to an adult faith that we take upon ourselves. This is what the residents of the village explained to the Samaritan woman who talked to them about Jesus: "It is no longer because of your words that we believe, for we have heard for ourselves, and we know that this is indeed the Savior of the world" (John 4:42).

As a cartoon expresses it: "God created everything! He even created the one who tries to prove that He does not exist.... This is to tell you that He is sure of Himself."[113] God wants us to look for Him because He wants us to find Him. He is always giving us discreet signs of His love and His presence. They are so discreet that we go by without seeing them.

Angels sometimes attract our attention with a friendly nudge. You walk with your eyes fixed on your feet or on the screen on your phone, but look! See the magnificent universe that the Lord created through love and that He gave you! See the brothers whom He put on your path to love and be loved by them! See that you are never alone, under the sun as well as under the storm, because He walks by your side.

The Angel Knows the Way

Everyone has a "companion" and a "protector" at his side that the Lord gives to man as an "aide" to get him to go forward when he stops and put him back on the right path

---

[113] Seen on Facebook — an illustration taken from the cartoon *Le Chat* [The cat].

when he takes the wrong road. But does man understand the richness of this gift? Above all, does he listen to the voice of this particular guardian?...

There is the danger of not going on the journey. And how many people settle down, and don't set out on the journey, and their whole life is stalled, without moving, without doing anything. It is a danger.... And so many people do not know how to make the journey, or are afraid of taking risks, and they are stalled....

But there is another danger, which is the danger of going astray.... Once, again, man is comforted by an absolute certainty: The angel is there to help us not to go astray.... The angel's reality is a reality that must be recognized. We must pray to him. Help me. The angel is authoritative. He has authority to guide us. But we must listen to him. We have to listen to the inspirations, which are always from the Holy Spirit—but the angel inspires them.

Do you speak with your angel?... Do you listen to your angel? Do you allow yourself to be led by the hand along the path, or do you need to be pushed to move?

For the angel's presence in our life does not simply help us on the road. It also assists us in seeing where we must arrive....

Our angel is not only with us; he also sees God the Father. He is in relationship with Him. He is the daily bridge, from the moment we arise to the moment we go to bed. He accompanies us and is a link between us and God the Father. The angel is the daily gateway to transcendence, to the encounter with the Father: that is, the angel helps me to go forward because he looks upon the Father, and he knows the way.[114]

"May the Lord give us all the grace to understand the mystery of the angel's protection," prays Pope Francis, "and of his companionship on the road and contemplation of God the Father."

---

[114] Francis, daily meditation, "The Angels, Our Traveling Companions."

16

Moving in the Night

I invite you to read this chapter while listening to
Jean-Philippe Rameau's "Hymne à la nuit" (Hymn
to the night), sung by a children's choir.

According to tradition, the Saracens attacked Christian homes
in Nazareth on the night of May 10, 1291. They drove away the
knights who were guarding the holy places and destroyed the
church that St. Helen had built over the house that had been
revealed to her as the place where the Annunciation occurred.
The humble home where the Son of God was incarnated in a
daughter of men was in danger of being reduced to dust. That
is when two angels seized the house and transported it, first to
Croatia, on the shores of Dalmatia, between Tersatz and Fiume.

At dawn, some butchers who were going to work noticed an
unknown building where, on the day before, there had been no
construction.

They were very astonished, approached the mysterious
building together, and examined it. It was a house that
was about thirty feet long and thirteen feet wide, was
built with small red square stones, and was very different

from the ones that people in the region were used to seeing.[115]

Bishop Alexander, who had been critically ill, arrived at the place, joyous and healthy. He bowed down in front of the house and profusely kissed its stone walls. Then he explained that the Virgin Mary had appeared to him during the night to reveal the origin of this house to him:

> This is where the Word became flesh.... The altar is the very one that St. Peter set up. The crucifix was placed there by my Son's disciples. The cedar statue is my true image, which was completed by St. Luke the Evangelist. God made this house pass from Nazareth to these shores so that it would not be subject to the desecration of the infidels, who had just invaded Galilee.[116]

Then, after being in Dalmatia for three and a half years, on the night of December 9–10, 1294, the Holy Family's house was removed in the same way to be transported all the way to central Italy, in the March of Ancona, which faces the Adriatic Sea. Some shepherds who were watching over their flocks saw a strange light come from above the sea and go down into a nearby forest.

Fr. Antoine Grillot believed that this miracle of the angels was a gift from Jesus to the Virgin Mary because of two memories that are connected to this place:

> When she lived on earth, the Virgin Mary preferred this modest house that reminded her of the Divine Child's

---

[115] Fr. Antoine Grillot, *La Sainte Maison de Lorette* [The Holy House in Loreto] (Tours: Alfred Mame et fils éditeurs, 1873), 18.
[116] Ibid., 19.

caresses. Must we be surprised that she carried this affection that she obtained from God up to the heavenly throne and one day commanded the angels, whose queen she was, to tear the remains of this precious home from the desecrated Asian soil and transport it beyond the seas to its new homeland?[117]

The place was named Loreto, either because of a woman named Lauretta, who had been the witness of these events, or because of a forest of bay laurels that was very close to it. It quickly became a place of pilgrimage and miracles. In 1460, a basilica was built there to enshrine the Holy Family's house.

The Holy Family's house was made of three stone walls that enclosed a grotto. They are the three walls that are now in Loreto, while the grotto is still venerated in Nazareth in the Basilica of the Annunciation. Each year on December 10, the feast of Our Lady of Loreto, the Church recalls the transportation of the Holy House.

Beloved Memories

How lovely it is to see that the Virgin Mary, like any mother, was attached to the childhood memories of her little Jesus! Some people who do not have emotional attachments to objects have a hard time understanding why you should keep children's first drawings, or a little bib, or a sweater that was knitted by a grandmother who passed away too soon.

Parents always think that time goes by too quickly. Even when they are delighted to see the solid, joyful teens or the magnificent adults that their children have become, they would love, for a

---

[117] Ibid., 28–29.

moment, to experience again their small bodies resting in their arms and the unique smell of their little heads nestling against their necks.

The miracle in Loreto tells us that Mary wanted to avoid the destruction of her childhood home, where Jesus took His first steps and said His first words, so that we, too, could meditate on the Son of God. He prayed and played like all the village children. He worked and traveled with His parents. He observed the world and life. Whether we be parents or teachers, we want to be loved by the children we are taking care of. But that is not where the criteria of a successful education is to be found.

The Upside-Down World

When I was in line at a grocery store, I overheard a dialogue between a lady and her grandson, who was sitting in a cart. The lady, who was talking a little loudly to make the people around her laugh, was saying:

"Did you *couri* [an invented word]? Are you sure you meant to say *couri*? Wouldn't it be *couru* [ran]?"

"No, Grandma, I *couri*."

"Ah, okay."

People around her were laughing. But I was not amused by the scene. It revealed too much of the shortcomings of today's education. We fail to correct children for fear that they might not take it well. Alas, this can lead to teenagers' being full of themselves and not trusting anyone. When this child discovers all by himself, when his friends mock him, that we say "*J'ai couru*" (I ran), how will he trust what his grandmother says? This failure to correct can also lead young adults to challenge rules.

Teachers suffer from this. They no longer transmit knowledge. They teach the child to do without teachers! "Today's education consists of accompanying the child in the discovery of his knowledge — as if he had an innate genius — and no longer of giving him knowledge."[118]

Today, we count too much on children's innate genius. We risk no longer giving them the fundamentals they need to shape their personalities. Jesus told us to pay attention to the house that is built without a foundation.

I cannot resist quoting this delightful dialogue of Alix de Saint-André about catechism reform in the 1970s:

"What did we teach these little ones, except for cutting out of the newspaper?"

"It is the inductive method, my Mother. We start from life, and children discover God, who is in their hearts..."

"Mother Antoinette, but the children do not discover anything. They invent, that's all! It has been two thousand years since we've known the answers, and we let them feel around? Wade in the twists and turns of their little mouse brains? Ah, that's charitable!"[119]

Frustration and Desire

As we saw earlier, to educate is to frustrate, or rather, it is to teach the child to manage his frustrations and to know how to delay

---

[118] Dr. Aldo Naouri, *Des bouts d'existence* [Bits and pieces of life], edited by Odile Jacob, 2019.

[119] Alix de Saint-André, *L'ange et le reservoir de liquide à freins* [The angel and the brake-fluid tank] (Paris: Gallimard, 1994), chap. 10. Let us also enjoy this sentence on the "restoration — excuse me, the renewal — of the Church" at this time: "That is when the archpriest emerged, dressed in blue overalls, like a laborer — except that a laborer would never come to church in blue overalls" (chap. 8).

things. I recently came across a lady with her three- or four-year-old son in the toy department. The child had chosen a toy. The mother took it out of the package to give it to him. She put the box in the shopping cart to pay for it. I was amazed. Either this is a technique to shop in peace, or we have reached the point where the child cannot even wait to get to the cash register before opening his gift.

We are no longer in the realm of impatience when it comes to a child who taps his foot to have a toy. We are in the very heart of desire. When there is no waiting, there is no desire. The time between the moment when the child chooses a toy in the store and the instant when the mother pays for it and gives it to him—it can be in the car or at home—is very important. The child is both frustrated and happy. He imagines all the opportunities for play that this toy offers him. He relishes his joy ahead of time. Incidentally, isn't this dreamed and anticipated joy often greater than the real joy that follows it? We end up finding the toy abandoned in a corner of the bedroom.

Desire is one of the most beautiful gifts that man was given to help him outdo himself and rise higher. When he is led only to egoistic pleasure, he becomes greedy. But when he opens himself up to others and to the world, what a powerful springboard!

Discipline: yet another word that makes you grind your teeth! In Latin, *disciplina* means "education." Here is advice that was given to first-grade teachers for the start of the school year in 2019 by Marie-Brigitte Lemaire, the founder of the Jean Qui Rit (John who laughs) method.[120]

What is your class atmosphere?
We can start working once discipline is there.

---

[120] See the blog *Pedágogie Jean Qui Rit*, JeanQuiRit.wordpress.com.

Consider your voice: Aren't you talking too fast? Loudly enough?

Have you thought of having the children relax during a moment of silence?

Are your gestures precise enough for reading?

Remember that the goal of these very structured lessons is to help your students to listen, look, do, and redo the gesture. Do not neglect a step.

For writing, how well do you work your right hand, your left hand, and both hands together?

Do you do dictation on the learning that just took place during reading?

Joy is part of teaching. But it does suppress effort.

When a child is weak, do you, above all, encourage him when he works well? After the endeavor, relaxation!

Children are already involved in what is most important for them. Movement is life.

Accept them as they are.

Everything is prepared for the child through this education. His eye looks, his ear hears, his gesture supports the sound that he hears, and rhythm organizes and coordinates the movement. Above all, imitate poetry. Once again, bravo for all that you do.

The Desire for God

Angels help us in this domain, for they are both the vision of God and the desire for Him. God is the only Being we continue to desire once we possess Him! The more we encounter Him, the more we feel like deepening this discovery and prolonging this encounter.

Little Thérèse is the saint of desire. She is the patron of missions without ever having left her little corner in Normandy.

Encounters with Angels

She needed only to cross the street—or almost—to go from the Buissonnets to the Carmel of Lisieux: "I am certain, then, that You will grant my desires; I know, O my God! that *the more You want to give, the more You make us desire.* I feel in my heart immense desires and it is with confidence I ask You to come and take possession of my soul." She wrote this in her "Offering to Merciful Love."

Giving our children the desire for God is the greatest gift we can offer them. When my children were small, prayer was at the heart of our family life. There was Sunday Mass, evening prayer, grace before meals, and intercessions for those who were going through hard times. Refusing to go to Mass started during adolescence. All the other practices were also abandoned for the sake of respecting their freedom and not seeming to be sectarian. But today, I'm aware that it's a pity! One of my daughters pointed it out to me recently. We have a testimony of faith to give our children. If our practice is too discreet in order not to bother them, we are not the witnesses that we should be. From whom will they receive what their parents do not transmit to them? They, of course, will find what they need in other places, and we, fortunately, do not know everything. But, at the level of faith, daily assimilation is necessary. Seeing us go to Mass is not enough. It is important for our children to notice that our faith is alive and active in our daily lives.

The Price of Life

A Jewish legend says that before their birth, children's souls are near God, and they know all His mysteries. Then God calls a soul and puts it in a body at the very beginning of its life. When he is born, the first person a child sees is his guardian angel. The angel says, "Hush" while placing his index finger on his mouth.

So the child forgets all heavenly secrets. The little depression on a person's upper lip is the print of the angel's finger. "At the end of eight days, when he was circumcised, he was called Jesus, the name given by the angel before he was conceived in the womb" (Luke 2:21).

Do we consult our child's guardian angel before calling him Myrtille or Terminator? Do we think of the heavenly groups that make this name resound all over Heaven? Glory to God for Virgule! Glory to God for Calimero! In Judaism, the name is the person's very identity. This is why some biblical characters changed their names. For example, in Genesis, Abram (meaning "the father is lifted up") became Abraham (the father of a multitude). Jacob (the one who took the place of another) became Israel (the one who struggled with God).

At the end of our lives, we will also receive a new name that will recapitulate all that we have become. "I will give him a white stone, with a new name written on the stone which no one knows except him who receives it" (Rev. 2:17).

Welcoming the Image and Finding the Resemblance

In his film, *Wings of Desire*,[121] Wim Wenders invites us to reflect on the body's beauty, through an angel who dreams of becoming a human person. When the angel becomes human, the movie changes from black and white to color. This disregards the splendors of Heaven, but it doesn't matter. It is beautiful to see this angel want to touch and feel. We have a body in order to love. Without a mouth, there is no kiss. Without a hand, there is no touch.

---

[121] 1987 Franco-German film.

The book of Genesis tell us that we are made "in the image and likeness of God." The Church Fathers commented on this expression in this way: We have the image of God in us. Nothing can delete it. Evil, our acts, and our refusal cannot do it. We have to reflect this resemblance day after day, through our goodwill, prayer, and love.

Jesus took on a human face through His Incarnation. He became like us. We recognize our miserable faces on His swollen, suffering, humiliated face. The Man of Sorrows became one of us. In His Passion, we recall the Transfiguration. Jesus' glorious face showed upon the Suffering Servant's tortured face. Glory and the Cross are intimately connected; they give each other meaning. Glory without the Cross is a too-distant power. The Cross without glory is the doorway to despair. God, who made Himself poor, became a little child, became a Man of Sorrows, and was condemned to death, permanently abolished the distance that separated us from Him.

This is why every life has meaning and a cost—even the one that seems the most useless. Ven. Marthe Robin, who became blind and disabled, was at first very isolated. Her life was futile before becoming so fruitful. Once that happened, she received hundreds of visitors in her dark little room.

Each of Us Is Unique

In her childhood, St. Thérèse of the Child Jesus and the Holy Face received a practical and attentive education from her mother and big sisters Pauline and Marie that was adapted to her character. One day, she wondered why, in Heaven, there were great saints who achieved heroic feats and little saints who had no incredible feats to their credit—only love and faithfulness. Her sister Pauline put a big glass and a thimble in front of her. She filled each with water and explained that holiness was letting yourself be filled with God's love. The volume did not matter. What mattered was to be full to the brim. Thérèse gladly took hold of this idea and found in it her "Little Way," which consists of instructions on holiness for very small souls.

Each child is unique. No ready-made recipe can work in education. We have to adapt our approach for a child who needs encouragement while her brother needs to have his impulses channeled. We have to adjust to another one who needs to abandon his thoughts in order to regain contact with reality and get his hands dirty, whereas we must help his sister to become introspective and get in touch with her feelings. Education that places the child at the heart of the system is a flexible education.

Each one of us is unique. Our role in the history of humanity is unique, whether it be well known or completely anonymous. Each life is precious. Every person is precious in God's eyes. "I praise you for I am fearfully and wonderfully made. Your eyes beheld my unformed substance" (see Ps. 139:14, 16).

Our role as Christian parents and educators is not to try to make our children love us. Our role is to give them the conviction that they are infinitely and unconditionally loved for who they are by this God of love who will never abandon them and who waits for them in order to fill them with His blessings.

Let us imagine that we are on the street. We see a man pass by, escorted by a bodyguard. We watch him and think: "Wow, he's a VIP—maybe a prince or a star!" Each one of us is this prince or princess whom a bodyguard escorts day and night. Our guardian angels are always at our sides. Doesn't our Heavenly Father show us how precious we are in His eyes since He commissioned these faithful servants of His to walk beside us?

Encounters with Angels

Compline Prayer

Visit, we beseech Thee, O Lord, this home,
and drive far from it all snares of the enemy;
let Thy holy angels dwell herein
to preserve us in peace,
and let Thy blessing always be upon us.
Through Christ, our Lord. Amen.

Children's Prayer to Their Guardian Angels

O my beautiful angel of light
Who is near me night and day,
Look at my soul in prayer
Which asks you for help:
Watch over me when I wake up,
Good angel, as God has said.
And each night when I am sleeping,
Bend over my little bed.

17

The Diplomatic Encounter

I invite you to read this chapter while listening to the
"Pontifical March" (a Vatican hymn) by Charles Gounod.

Becoming a successor of St. Peter is such a heavy burden that
many prelates do not want it! On October 14, 1978, Cardinal
Karol Wojtyla saw his name appear in the election as of the first
day. He was tense and worried and not expecting that. The situation in his country, Poland, was already so explosive. Hadn't he
come to the conclave, incidentally, with a simple tourist visa?
The authorities had taken away his diplomatic passport because
he had come to Rome a month earlier for the election of John
Paul I, the "smiling pope." But John Paul I's pontificate lasted
only thirty-three days. It was interrupted on September 28 by
his unexpected death.

That very evening, Msgr. Wyszynski, Poland's primate, went
into the room of the young archbishop of Krakow. He told him
that "the new pope's task will be to have the Church enter into
the third millennium. I come to encourage you. Accept this
mission that the Lord has given you." The next day, while he
was going toward the Sistine Chapel for the continuation of the
votes and debates, Cardinal Maximilian de Fürstenberg, one

of Cardinal Wojtyla's oldest friends, whispered some words to him: "The Teacher is here and is calling you" (see John 11:28). Cardinal Wojtyla was elected that afternoon and was called John Paul II.

It was an overwhelming task. But the sovereign pontiff did not bear it alone. Veronica Giuliani, an eighteenth-century Italian Poor Clare nun, thought that when a new pope was elected, he received twelve angels who would protect the Church during his pontificate.

Many popes have relied on angels' help. Pius XI, a contemporary of Stalin, Hitler, and Mussolini, invoked the guardian angel of the person he was speaking to when he feared a difficult interview:

> During a conversation that I had with the extraordinary Pope Pius XI, I heard him expound on a very beautiful secret. It confirmed that the guardian angel's protection always brought joy, settled all difficulties, and decreased obstacles. Pius XI confided to me: "When I have to talk to an unreasonable person I have to persuade in some way, I advise my guardian angel to keep the person whom I have to meet up to date on everything. In this way, once the agreement between the two superior minds was completed, the conference took place in the best conditions and was facilitated."[122]

His successor, Pius XII, who was called the "angelic pastor," the "doctor of peace," and the "angel of charity," exhorted the

---

[122] John XXIII alluding to Pope Pius XI, address in the Basilica of Saint Mary of the Angels, September 9, 1962.

faithful to be familiar with their guardian angels. He explained that there was "another world that was invisible, but just as real as ours."[123] The Holy Father saw our guardian angels as our fellow travelers who work for our sanctification by fostering our intimacy with God. He said:

> [The angels] have been given the task of keeping careful watch over you so that you do not become separated from Christ, their Lord. And not only do they want to protect you from the dangers which waylay you throughout your journey: they are actually by your side, helping your souls as you strive to go ever higher in your union with God through Christ....
>
> Have a certain familiarly with the angels, who are forever solicitous for your salvation and your sanctification. If God wishes, you will spend a happy eternity with the angels: get to know them here, from now on.[124]

John XXIII always repeated: "My good angel inspired me with this or that." In his diary, he wrote: "An angel of Paradise is always beside me." He believed that our guardian angels accompany us in prayer in order for our prayer to bear more fruit:

> We ask our guardian angel in particular to assist us in the daily recitation of the Divine Office in order to recite it with dignity, attention, and devotion so that it may become pleasing to God, fruitful for us and the souls of others.[125]

---

[123] Pius XII, address, October 3, 1958.
[124] Ibid.
[125] John XXIII, apostolic exhortation *Sacrae laudis* (January 6, 1962).

Encounters with Angels

Each of us has his own guardian angel, and every one of us can converse with the guardian angels of others.[126]

The one who was nicknamed "the good pope" prayed to his angel at least five times a day:

How consoling it is to feel that this heavenly guardian angel, this guide to our footsteps, and this witness of our most intimate actions, is right near us. I recite the prayer: "Angel of God, my guardian dear" at least five times a day. I often engage in spiritual conversations with him. They are always calm and peaceful.[127]

This is a prayer from the eighteenth century:

Angel of God, my guardian dear,
To whom God's love commits me here,
Ever this day, be at my side,
To light and guard,
To rule and guide.
Amen.[128]

St. John Paul II recommended this: "Feel the angels' presence near you, and let yourselves be guided by them."[129] "Thinking about and venerating angels helps us to approach the thrice-holy and invisible God. We will, along with them, see Him face-to-face in the Kingdom of God."

---

[126] John XXIII, *L'Osservatore Romano*, weekly French edition, no. 33, August 9, 1961.

[127] John XXIII, letter to his niece Sr. Angela Roncali, October 3, 1948.

[128] Pius VI, September 20, 1796.

[129] John Paul II, September 29, 2004.

The German pope Benedict XVI invited us to be inspired by angels to become angels to each other:

The Angel is a creature who stands before God, oriented to God with his whole being. All three names of the Archangels end with the word "*El*", which means "God". God is inscribed in their names, in their nature. Their true nature is existing in his sight and for him. In this very way the second aspect that characterizes Angels is also explained: they are God's messengers. They bring God to men, they open heaven and thus open earth. Precisely because they are with God, they can also be very close to man. Indeed, God is closer to each one of us than we ourselves are. The Angels speak to man of what constitutes his true being, of what in his life is so often concealed and buried. They bring him back to himself, touching him on God's behalf. In this sense, we human beings must also always return to being angels to one another — angels who turn people away from erroneous ways and direct them always, ever anew, to God.[130]

Dear friends, the Lord is ever close and active in humanity's history and accompanies us with the unique presence of his Angels, whom today the Church venerates as "Guardian Angels", that is, ministers of the divine care for every human being.[131]

Pope Francis shakes us up by inviting us to question ourselves on the condition of our relationship with our guardian angel:

[130] Benedict XVI, homily, September 29, 2007.
[131] Benedict XVI, Angelus, October 2, 2011.

Encounters with Angels

Today, I would ask myself this question: How is my relationship with my guardian angel? Do I listen to him? Do I bid him good day in the morning? Do I tell him: "Guard me while I sleep"? Do I speak with him? Do I ask his advice? He is beside me. We can answer these questions today. How is my relationship with this angel that the Lord has sent to guard me and to accompany me on the path, and who always beholds the face of the Father who is in heaven?[132]

So that we are never left alone, God has put at each person's side a guardian angel to support and protect us, to accompany us in life. It is up to us to perceive his presence, listening to his advice, with the docility of a child, in order to keep ourselves on the right path toward paradise.... Our guardian angel "is always with us and this is a reality: he is like an ambassador of God with us".[133]

The Love of the Church

Quoting a Rwandan proverb, Fr. Daniel-Ange said that "when the devil throws stones against the Church, the angels pick them up to continue building it!" We all have criticisms to make about the Church — e.g., an unpleasant memory, a bad example, a priest who did not know how to make us feel welcome during a difficult confession, a homily that shocked us, a woman who rebuked us for coming to Mass with a baby, a gloomy and silent assembly, a sacristan who criticizes everything and everyone. We have experienced authentic wounds to our self-esteem. Nonetheless,

---

[132] Francis, homily, October 2, 2014.
[133] Francis, morning meditation, October 2, 2015.

the Church is you and I, as Mother Teresa said to a journalist! It will change by us and with us. Above all, it will not be built without us.

Will We Flee?

In Taizé,[134] I received the keen awareness of belonging to the Church as the Body of Christ. When I discovered the Church's "little springtime" in 1986, my first generous adolescent thought was that my neighborhood church did not welcome people with open arms in its ecclesiastical goodwill, and I found the Taizé community "so much better than in a parish!" But the brothers in Taizé did not see it this way. All the teachings and group discussions sent us firmly back to our own parishes. Br. Roger himself wrote:

> Thoughtlessness sometimes creeps into this communion of love, which is the Body of Christ, His Church. This causes a lot of suffering. So, are we going to flee? No, never. We can only run to support renewal among God's people.

These words disturbed us and shook us up. If our parish does not meet our expectations, we can stand idly by, complaining and finding believers around us who share our dissatisfaction. We can go and see if the grass is greener and the songs are more dynamic elsewhere. Or we can begin and support a renewal that we want. This can take many forms: starting an Alpha course, offering an evening of praise or adoration of the Blessed Sacrament from time to time, joining the marriage preparation team

---

[134] The Taizé community is an ecumenical Christian monastic fraternity in Taizé, Saône-et-Loire, Burgundy, France, founded in 1940 by Roger Louis Schutz-Marsauche, known as Br. Roger. —Ed.

to rejuvenate it if it is struggling, starting a choir with some volunteers to support a leader who is trying to pass on her joy in singing for God by herself, or forming a little core group to lead a monthly family Mass in which teens and young children would take on roles. I am sure that there are many other ideas that are dear to your heart. There are so many good initiatives, such as the Parish System of Evangelization Cells, which celebrated its thirtieth anniversary in November 2019, and the Perpetual Eucharistic Adoration movements.

We will to have to be patient. Sometimes this will take several months—even two or three years. We will be serene and persevering, confident, and joyous. We will be interested in other parish activities and participate in key moments. Perhaps we will have to suffer from the thoughtlessness of this or that person or from the system's very functioning. But we will hang in there.

Run away? Never! To whom would we go? Jesus Himself built the Church while promising us that the gates of Hades would not prevail against it. This promise was entrusted to us. It is up to us to roll up our sleeves to make it thrive and shine.

The Pentecost of Love

In 1936, Marthe Robin announced a renewal of French parish life that she named "the New Pentecost of love." A friend, the philosopher Jean Guitton, asked her one day how this would manifest itself. Marthe said:

Oh! Not in an extraordinary way. I see it as peaceful and slow. I think that this will be gradually done. I even believe that it has already started. As for the future, you know that people give me a lot of ideas about the future. I do not know anything except for one thing. The future is Jesus.

In the book of Revelation, there is one angel for each church:

> Write what you see in a book and send it to the seven churches.... On turning I saw seven golden lampstands, and in the midst of the lampstands one like a son of man, clothed with a long robe and with a golden girdle round his breast.... In his right hand he held seven stars.... "As for the mystery of the seven stars which you saw in my right hand, and the seven golden lampstands, the seven stars are the angels of the seven churches and the seven lampstands are the seven churches." (1:11–12, 16, 20)

So it is with the angel of each of our parishes. We can invoke him when we think that our parish community is lacking enthusiasm, charity, and evangelical zeal, in order for him to inspire us with solutions.

The Angels' Voices

Fr. Jean-Édouard Lamy, who was a priest in La Courneuve at the beginning of the twentieth century, heard angel voices in his church. One day, they made him give up cleaning the church windows, which were about to explode, and thus saved his life.

> I thought my church windows were very dirty. I wanted to clean them. But I heard the Archangel Gabriel and my angel talking to each other and saying: "It's not necessary." So I did not do it. Very often, when they want to teach me good lessons, they talk to each other and let me hear their conversation. A few hours later, after the catastrophe [the explosion of an ammunition dump], those windows burst in shards. I was very inspired and might have stayed in the church for a long time. Then I had an inspiration that

surely came to me from the angels: I did not stay to pray for an hour, a half hour, or even minutes; I left for Paris to buy some souvenirs for the First Communicants. Shortly after I left, everything exploded. The vault collapsed, and cartloads of tiles fell.[135]

Fr. Lamy sometimes saw St. Gabriel and entrusted him with messages: "I am making him responsible for my messages for the Blessed Virgin Mary. I say to him: 'So, tell her this and that.' He does not answer, but he smiles."

Fr. Lamy advised us to pray to the angels more often. "We do not pray to our guardian angels frequently enough. We do not consider them to be as important as they are. We do not pray to them enough! Angels are very touched when we pray to them."

Origen wrote in the third century:

I do not hesitate to think angels are also present in our assembly since they watch over not only the whole Church but each one of us as well.

Prayer

You are my guardian.
Because I have confided
In your celestial goodness,
Enlighten me,
Take care of me,
Rule over me! Amen.

— Prayer of Pope John XXIII

---

[135] Paul Biver, *Apôtre et mystique* [Apostle and mystic] (Paris: Éditions du Serviteur, 2000).

18

The Intercession Encounter

I invite you to read this chapter while listening to *God's Saints* from the Emmanuel Community (2013).

Abraham and his family, his servants, and his flocks had set up their camp not far from Hebron, in the plain of Mamre, under the oak trees. During the hottest part of the day, Abraham was seated at the entrance of the tent when he noticed three men approaching him. He ran to meet them and bowed down to the ground.

"My lord, if I have found favor in your sight, do not pass by your servant. Let a little water be brought, and wash your feet, and rest yourselves under the tree, while I fetch a morsel of bread, that you may refresh yourselves, and after that you may pass on — since you have come to your servant."

"Very well," they answered, "do as you have said."

Later, they got up to leave and headed toward Sodom. Abraham escorted them for a while. While "the Lord" stayed near Abraham to tell him about the destruction of Sodom and Gomorrah, "the two angels" continued going toward Sodom.

Abraham started up a long negotiation with God to try to save the city and its residents:

"Wilt thou indeed destroy the righteous with the wicked? Suppose there are fifty righteous within the city; wilt thou then destroy the place and not spare it for the fifty righteous who are in it? Far be it from thee to do such a thing, to slay the righteous with the wicked, so that the righteous fare as the wicked! Far be that from thee! Shall not the Judge of all the earth do right?"

"If I find at Sodom fifty righteous in the city, I will spare the whole place for their sake."

"I have taken upon myself to speak to the Lord, I who am but dust and ashes. Suppose five of the fifty righteous are lacking? Wilt thou destroy the whole city for lack of five?"

"I will not destroy it if I find forty-five there."

"Suppose forty are found there."

"For the sake of forty I will not do it."

"Oh, let not the Lord be angry, and I will speak. Suppose thirty are found there."

"I will not do it, if I find thirty there."

"Behold, I have taken upon myself to speak to the Lord. Suppose twenty are found there."

"For the sake of twenty I will not destroy it."

"Oh, let not the Lord be angry, and I will speak again but this once. Suppose ten are found there."

"For the sake of ten I will not destroy it."

This concludes the dialogue between God and Abraham. It is why ten adult men are needed in Judaism to recite prayers during services or ceremonies.[136]

---

[136] Read this story in Genesis 18:1–5, 16–33.

Praying for Those We Love

In Victor Hugo's *Les Misérables*, we find the beautiful and holy figure of the bishop of Digne.[137]

"Madame Magloire," said the Bishop, "place those things as near the fire as possible." And turning to his guest: "The night wind is harsh on the Alps. You must be cold, sir."

Each time that he uttered the word *sir*, in his voice which was so gently grave and polished, the man's face lighted up. *Monsieur* to a convict is like a glass of water to one of the shipwrecked of the *Medusa*. Ignominy thirsts for consideration.

"This lamp gives a very bad light," said the Bishop.

Madame Magloire understood him, and went to get the two silver candlesticks from the chimney-piece in Monseigneur's bed-chamber, and placed them, lighted, on the table.

"Monsieur le Curé," said the man, "you are good; you do not despise me. You receive me into your house. You light your candles for me. Yet I have not concealed from you whence I come and that I am an unfortunate man."

The Bishop, who was sitting close to him, gently touched his hand. "You could not help telling me who you were. This is not my house; it is the house of Jesus Christ. This door does not demand of him who enters whether he has a name, but whether he has a grief. You suffer, you are hungry and thirsty; you are welcome. And do not

---

[137] For the character of Msgr. Myriel, Victor Hugo was inspired by Msgr. De Miollis, who was the bishop of Digne from 1805 to 1838. They both had the nickname Bienvenu (Welcome).

thank me; do not say that I receive you in my house. No one is at home here, except the man who needs a refuge. I say to you, who are passing by, that you are much more at home here than I am myself. Everything here is yours. What need have I to know your name? Besides, before you told me you had one which I knew."

The man opened his eyes in astonishment.

"Really? You knew what I was called?"

"Yes," replied the Bishop, "you are called my brother."[138]

Nonetheless, let's not make the wrong friends! Here's a funny post, as we often read from those who are resistant to excessive networking:

"Hello,

As I do not have Facebook, I try to make friends outside the real Facebook but by applying the same principles: Every day, I go out on the street, and I explain to the passersby what I ate, how I'm feeling, what I did the day before, what I'm doing now, and what I'll do tomorrow.

I give them pictures of my wife, my dog, my children, of myself washing the car, and of my wife sewing. I also listen to their conversations, and I say, "I love you."

That works. I already have 4 followers—2 police officers, 1 psychiatrist, and 1 psychologist.

Our loved ones, family, and friends are the ones we hug; they are counting on us, and we are able to count on them. Besides

---

[138] Victor Hugo, *Les Misérables*, trans. Isabel F. Hapgood (New York: Thomas Y. Crowell, 1887), vol. 1, bk. 2, chap. 3.

these, there are others, known and unknown, who need us. We will be their angels, sometimes without knowing it. Jesus asked the lawyer, "Which of these three, do you think, proved neighbor to the man who fell among the robbers?" He said, "The one who showed mercy on him." And Jesus said to him, "Go and do likewise" (Luke 10:36–37).

Knowing How to Give and Receive

Angels help us a lot. But sometimes they ask for help, as if to show us the joy of giving and also the grace of receiving.

One day, Agnes of Langeac was praying in a church when "a small child with charming grace" approached her and begged for money. Agnes had nothing but could not let him leave empty-handed. She saw a silver coin on the ground. Before giving it to the child, she asked him if he knew how to make the Sign of the Cross. "Oh yes, very well!" said the little child with a smile. Then he disappeared. He was an angel.

St. Gregory the Great was born in Rome around 540. He grew up in a rich family. After his parents died, he gave all his goods to the poor and kept only a silver bowl in memory of his mother. A beggar appeared before him. He was a merchant who had lost all his wealth in a shipwreck and begged him to help him. Gregory gave him the twelve coins that he possessed. Since that was not enough, he gave him his bowl.

When he became pope, he asked his chaplain to organize a dinner by inviting twelve poor people to represent the twelve apostles. That night, he sat at the table with them and criticized the chaplain for having invited thirteen people. The unhappy chaplain re-counted the guests and assured the pope that there were only twelve of them. Gregory understood that he was the only one who saw the thirteenth guest, who sometimes took on the appearance of a young man and sometimes that of an elderly man. After the meal, Gregory took his hand and led him into his apartments to question him. The man said to him:

"Do you remember that unfortunate merchant to whom you gave twelve crowns and the silver bowl that you possessed? Believe that it was for this work that God wanted you to become St. Peter's successor. You are his faithful imitator because of your charity toward the poor."

The astonished Gregory asked: "How do you know that?"

"Because I am the angel whom God had sent to test you. But do not fear. I am watching over you. God sent me to protect you to the end and to grant you everything you ask for."

Each one of us, even the poorest of the poor, has angels watching over him. The angels are glorious, pure, and splendid, but they have been given to us as companions along the way of life. They have the task of watching over you all, so that you do not stray away from Christ, your Lord.[139]

Confidence in the Future

Scaremongering predictions have never been lacking and will always exist. For example, Yves Cochet, a former minister of the environment, became a "radical collapsologist." Dating back to 2015, collapsology is a new discipline that studies the collapse of industrial civilization. It covers many fields, including ecology, economics, anthropology, geopolitics, demography, health, and so forth. In September 2019, Cochet announced on Twitter, "In the next thirty years, 50 percent of humanity will die." It's possible!

---

[139] Pius XII, meeting with American pilgrims, October 3, 1958.

Humanity is able to destroy itself in the next thirty minutes. Humanity can also do good, make the world a better place, dig wells, develop vaccines, heal wounded bodies, and bring joy and beauty into our lives. Angels invite us to look beyond our daily worries and have a panoramic outlook. All parents have had this experience. When we have very young children and are overwhelmed by daily hardships, we want time to go by faster. But then, when we see those children grow up and spread their wings, how we wish we had made the most of every second! We have only the present moment to express our love to others and to God. Let us not let this grace go by.

Jacques d'Arnoux, a writer and fighter pilot during the First World War, had a serious spinal injury in 1917. Thanks to his willpower, he managed to walk again for five years and wrote about the importance of living in the present moment: "This striking vocation of the present moment is the most beautiful and divine one that can be offered to us. The one who does not know how to follow it with all his will is not worthy of the heroic life."

"Happiness for All Those I Love"

St. John Bosco thought that our guardian angels' desire to help us is much greater than our desire to be helped by them. So let us not fear to tire them with our requests and prayers. Our angels do not have contradictory spirits. The more we entrust our loved ones to them, the more they will watch over our loved ones.

Il Grigio, "the Gray One" — this is what St. John Bosco called the big fierce dog that appeared when he wandered through the disreputable alleyways in Turin for his ministry. A strong anti-clerical climate prevailed then. Priests were often attacked. One day, a man fired two shots at Don Bosco and missed him. The man then tried to fall on him. But the enormous dog intervened, and the attacker fled. Another time, two men came from behind Don Bosco and threw a bag over his head. The dog immediately emerged out of nowhere. One of the thugs ran for his life, whereas the other one, who was terrified, was kept at bay by the animal until John Bosco asked him to let the thug go.

When asked what he thought about the dog, Don Bosco said that to say it was an angel was laughable. But we cannot say that it was an ordinary dog either.

Marcel Van humorously described the protection of his angel, who made himself his bodyguard, as if he were an important person:

Guardian angel, my brother, you are always beside me, right? As a bodyguard, help me to be careful. Although I am not president, the furious demon does not stop wanting to assassinate me. I think that, without his presence, your little brother would be in a lot of danger. So I always count on you.[140]

Some of you may have sung this old Christmas song, which has always moved me:

Three angels came tonight
To bring me beautiful things.
One of them had a censer;
The other had a hat of roses.

On that Christmas night, the angels suggested that the person ask for what he wanted:

---

[140] Marie-Michel, "Notes Intimes" [Intimate notes] in *L'amour me connaît. Écrits spirituels de Marcel Van* [Love knows me. spiritual writings of Marcel Van] (Paris: Le Sarment-Fayard, 1990).

Christmas, Christmas, I am bringing
What you want from Heaven
For the good Lord, who is in the depths
of the blue sky,
Is sad when you sigh.

The angels then offered him better gifts: a lovely golden censer, a crown of roses, a robe similar to the Virgin Mary's, a silver necklace, fruits of Paradise, or even to see the Child Jesus in His swaddling clothes in the manger. This would be the ultimate joy, as it was for the shepherds.

Christmas, Christmas, return to Heaven,
My beautiful angels, in this very moment
In the blue sky, ask God to ensure that
The one I love is happy.

The melody also works if we say:

In the blue sky, ask God to ensure
That all those I love are happy.

Prayer

Let us learn this prayer of St. Francis de Sales, which we can recite for all those we love.

O holy guardian angels of my good parents [spouse and children], dear friends, benefactors, and beloved and faithful servants, I beg you to surround them with your heavenly protection at all times by vigilantly sheltering them under your chaste wings so that they would be well protected from every sin and affliction. Helpful angels, I beseech you to enable them to be spiritually and physically healthy. Amen.

19

The Encounter with New Life

I invite you to read this chapter while listening to the Taizé
Community's Resurrection songs: "Christus Resurrexit,"
"Surrexit Christus," "Surrexit Dominus Vere," and so forth.

First, it was the Sabbath rest—the great silence of Holy Saturday.
There was the astonishment that follows big tragic events, when
we have cried and shouted too much and are unable to be silent
in the face of the rubble of our shattered lives.

On the morning of the third day, the dawn's white light pierced
the night. A bird let his song be heard. Some women were rush-
ing. Their love was stronger than the dark, the fear, the void, and
the terror. They sang the blessing that every Jewish man recited
when they awoke: "I thank You, O living and eternal King, in
Your goodness, for having given my soul back to me."[141]

They held tightly the pots that contained spices. The fragrance
of the myrrh mingled with the scent of the flowering trees. To
think that it was necessary to abandon the bruised body without

---

[141] Modé (for the man; the woman says "Moda") ani léfanekha
mélekh'haï vekayam chéhé'hézarta bi nichmati be'hemla raba
émounatékha.

even washing the blood and dust from it. There was hardly time to embalm it with a mix of myrrh and aloes to preserve it until now. He had not been buried near His father Joseph, since convicts did not have the right to rest in their ancestors' tomb. This was one more humiliation that, strangely, did not seem to affect His Mother. With the shadow of a smile, she only whispered: "Oh, the tomb."

"Will there be Roman soldiers?"

"Who will roll away the stone for us?"

"Shh, here we are."

"Mary, there are Temple guards!"

The day had dawned. The sun's rising light bathed the garden. The Jewish guards and the women who looked at each other from a distance were defensive. They were all equally worried. Suddenly, the earth trembled, and the landscape was undulating.

"Mary!"

The women, standing close together, held their breath. Two nights ago, Mary Magdalene and Mary the mother of James and Joseph, with the courage of their silent and persistent tenderness, had been the last ones to leave the sealed tomb; they had stayed until the last lights of the Sabbath forced them to return home.

The ground started to tremble again in the calm of this silent dawn. The guards' coarse words reached them without their heeding them, for the bright light had nothing to do with the sun. There was an angel in front of the tomb. He seemed to be made of the same material as the light. He rolled back the stone and sat on it, while the Temple guards fell to the ground, as if they were dead. How soft the angel's face looked — and wasn't it also admirable? — when he spoke to the trembling women:

"Do not be amazed; you seek Jesus of Nazareth, who was crucified. He has risen, he is not here; see the place where they laid him" (Mark 16:6).

They reached the tomb together and went into it. It was empty. The linen wrappings that were used for the hasty burial were laid in their place on the light stone, as if nothing had disturbed them. If He is not here, then where is He?

The angel said: "Go quickly and tell his disciples that he has risen from the dead, and behold, he is going before you to Galilee; there you will see him" (Matt. 28:7).

They abandoned their spices and all they had prepared for the anointing of the body and left the garden. Their joy had not yet driven away the anxiety. Where was He? Where was the one they loved?

Mary Magdalene stopped so abruptly that her companion bumped into her. A man was standing on the path in front of them.

"Greetings."

At these words, the doubts were gone. It was really His voice! His appearance surprised them. He was so majestic, but it was really His voice and His look! They fell to their knees, grabbed His feet, and covered them with kisses. Oh! Those wounds, which were still visible but radiating light—this mystery that could be seen. Divine life was supporting this tortured body, filling it, and inhabiting it.

"Do not be afraid; go and tell my brothers to go to Galilee; there they will see me."

He was no longer there. After three years of following and learning from Him, the time had come for them to take up the mission.

"Let's go see Peter!"

Encounters with Angels

When they crossed the city gate, they were overtaken by the guards, who ran toward the Temple to announce the news to the high priest.

Faith in the Resurrection

It is really difficult to find consistency in the chronology of the different accounts of the Resurrection! We can see it in the films that trace Jesus' life. The Resurrection is always the most disappointing moment.

In Matthew (28:1–11), there was an earthquake. Then an angel who looked like a lightning bolt rolled away the stone and sat on it before speaking to the two women—Mary Magdalene and Mary the mother of James and Joseph. They were going to speak to the apostles, who were immediately leaving for Galilee.

In Mark (16:1–8), there are three of them—Mary Magdalene, Mary the mother of James, and Salome. The stone had been rolled back. The women went into the tomb, and an angel who looked like a young man was sitting in it—to the right. (Jewish tombs are as large as a room, with hollow spaces in the stone.) The women fled and said nothing to anybody because they were afraid.

In Luke (24:1–11), we meet Mary Magdalene and Mary the mother of James, with Joanna and "another woman with them." They found that the stone was rolled back. They went in and saw nothing. Then two angels in dazzling clothes appeared to them and asked them why they were looking for the living among the dead. They told this to the apostles, who did not believe them. Peter was the only one to run to the tomb. He came back amazed.

In John (20:11–18), Mary Magdalene was the only one. It was still dark. She saw that the stone had been taken away. She ran to alert Peter and John, who went and found that the linen wrappings were lying there. When they left, she bent over and, crying, peered into the tomb. She saw "two angels in white, sitting where the body of Jesus had lain, one at the head and one at the feet." They asked her why she was crying. Then Jesus appeared.

> The voice of the angel
> Was in the secret of our hearts
> In the Lord's empty tomb.[142]

Why did Jesus first appear to the women? St. Thomas Aquinas gave us two reasons:[143]

1. *To wipe out the ancestral shame.* "Christ appeared to the woman first, for this reason, that as a woman was the first to bring the source of death to man, so she might be the first to announce the dawn of Christ's glorious Resurrection. Hence Cyril says on John 20:17: 'Woman who formerly was the minister of death, is the first to see and proclaim the adorable mystery of the Resurrection: thus womankind has procured absolution from ignominy, and removal of the curse.'"

2. *To reward faithfulness.* "The women whose love for our Lord was more persistent—so much so that 'when even the disciples withdrew' from the sepulchre 'they did not depart' [Gregory, *Hom. xxv in Evang.*]—were the first to see Him rising in glory."

Mastering Death Again

Dr. Aldo Naouri, a famous pediatrician and psychologist, developed a very interesting point of view in this regard:

---

[142] An Easter-season hymn.
[143] Thomas Aquinas, *Summa Theologica*, IIIa, q. 55, art. 1, reply to obj. 3.

The problem goes back to World War II. The Holocaust and the atomic bomb, with the awareness that humanity was capable of destroying itself, led to a real horror of death. Before 1945, death was a part of life.... After 1945, the process was reversed. We do not think that death is as important. We do not make the Sign of the Cross in front of the hearse. We neglect cemeteries. Modern society trivializes murder and death to such an extent that it makes them unreal.[144]

Saints believe that death is not a separation, but a reunion. St. Thérèse of the Child Jesus and the Holy Face transmitted this filial confidence to us. She wrote:

It's not "death" that will come in search of me, it's God. Death isn't some phantom, some horrible spectre, as it is represented in pictures. It is said in the catechism that "death is the separation of the soul from the body" and that is all it is.[145]

She also said: "Yes, I'm like a tired and harassed traveler, who reaches the end of his journey and falls over. Yes, but I'll be falling into God's arms."[146] Angels, including our guardian angels, will help us on this passage, as if we were crossing rivers or brambles.

Having seen him next to her all her life, St. Frances of Rome was not abandoned by her guardian angel when she died on

---

[144] Aldo Naouri, "On ne peut être que des parents imparfaits" [We can only be imperfect parents], interview in *Famille chrétienne*, no. 2159, June 1–7, 2019, 37.
[145] Thérèse of the Child Jesus and the Holy Face, *Her Last Conversations*, Yellow Notebook, May 1, 1897.
[146] Ibid., September 15, 1897.

March 9, 1440: "Heaven opened up, the angels came down, and the archangel finished his task. He was standing in front of me and motioned me to follow him."

The young Anne de Guigné did not see angels generally, but she could see hers before she died: "Very true, very true, he is there! I see him, Mommy. He is there! Turn around. You will also see him! How beautiful he is!" She was a rebellious and irascible little girl who became a model of obedience for the love of Jesus. She asked the nun who was taking care of her to be permitted to die:

"Sister, may I go with the angels?"

"Yes, my beautiful little girl," the nun said.

"Thank you, Sister! Oh, thank you!"

St. Vincent Ferrer, who preached about the end times, slowly died on the Wednesday of Holy Week, on April 5, 1419, around four o'clock in the afternoon. At that very moment, a cloud of small white butterflies came into his room.

"Look!" someone exclaimed. "These are angels who are coming to get Vincent's soul to lead him straight to Paradise."

Let us conclude with St. Joseph, whom we call the patron of a happy death. He left this world in the presence of Mary and Jesus. The angels had already taught him to leave everything behind:

- his certainty when he was invited to take Mary, his pregnant wife, into his home
- the city of Bethlehem when Herod was looking for the Child to put Him to death
- Egypt's security when those who resented the Child died

Being an obedient and humble man, by following the angels' advice, he guided the Holy Family that was entrusted to him in the best possible way.

Encounters with Angels

Fear and Astonishment

When the Resurrection was announced, the apostles, even more than the women, were disturbed, perplexed, worried, and doubtful. The feeling that perhaps best expresses the inexpressible nature of the Resurrection is astonishment. "Faith, like life, becomes dull and routine without astonishment.[147] We believe, but not to the point of longing for the new life that awaits us. We love Jesus, but not to the extent that we wish to meet Him. Yet should we not be preparing a little bit now for this condition, which will be our eternity? In this way, our astonishment will give way to the eternal joy that Jesus promised us!

The Resurrection is for us! Jesus died by giving His life for us. But God also raised Him up for us. It is our promise and our gift. "We bring you the good news that what God promised to the fathers, this he has fulfilled to us their children by raising Jesus" (Acts 13:32–33).

This has immediate consequences. We do not live by waiting for death, let alone by killing ourselves, as some cult followers have believed. The Resurrection bears its seeds of life in this world:

> The resurrection of Christ is the principle of new life for every man and every woman, for true renewal always begins from the heart, from the conscience. Yet Easter is also the beginning of the new world, set free from the slavery of sin and death: the world open at last to the Kingdom of God, a Kingdom of love, peace and fraternity.[148]

Being messengers of God, angels are present during the two great moments of salvation history. An angel announced the

---

[147] Francis, tweet, June 4, 2019.
[148] Francis, Easter message, April 21, 2019.

coming of Jesus at the Annunciation, and angels proclaimed the victory of life over death and the end of the curse!

For the first time, these words are pronounced: "He is risen". A superior being was needed. This was because for the human being, this truth and these words, which communicate this truth — "He is risen" — this very truth is so overwhelming and unbelievable that perhaps no man would have dared to say it.[149]

Angels are at the gates of both worlds. When we are in trouble, they remind us that it will not last forever and that all our sufferings are compensated for in Heaven. When we are joyous, they tell us that this joy is real and holy because it reflects what we will experience in an eternity of love. "Be not afraid!" You are moving not toward a void but toward the greatest love.

Meditation

The very Resurrection of Christ must not be directly seen by men, but be announced by the angels.[150]

An angel first announced the Resurrection in order to be the messenger of God's will to proclaim the Resurrection.[151]

"A Sailboat Goes By"

I am standing upon the seashore,
A ship sails to the morning breeze
and starts for the blue ocean.

---

[149] John Paul II, April 1, 1991.
[150] Thomas Aquinas, *Summa Theologica*, III, q. 55, art. 2, conclusion.
[151] Hilary of Poitiers, quoted in ibid.

Encounters with Angels

She is an object of beauty and strength.
I stand and watch her
till at last she fades
on the horizon ...
and just at the moment when someone at
   my side says,
"There, she is gone!"
there are other eyes watching her coming,
and other voices ready to take up the glad shout.
"There she comes!"
There are no dead.
There are living people on both shores.

                   —Unknown

The Last Encounter: Thousands
of Celebrating Angels

I do not hesitate to invite you to end this book by
listening to Handel's "Hallelujah Chorus," the most
famous chorus in his oratorio Messiah. It's true, it's
perhaps a bit trite, but during this time of listening
and reading, let us put our worries aside. May we enjoy
the truth of Jesus' Resurrection. Let us receive His
promise: eternal life with God and all those we love.

Death came looking for her like a friend, toward the end of a very
full day. She peacefully fell asleep while joyfully looking toward
the future. Death had not been able to hold back her only Son
in her arms. It did not hold back the Mother of God either. Mary
had hardly gone to sleep when Jesus plucked her like the most
beautiful rose in the garden. He took her up "body and soul into
heavenly glory" (CCC 966). Corruption would not touch the
body that received and carried Him, the arms that rocked Him,
the lips that smiled at Him, or the hands that served Him. He
welcomed her and crowned her. She is the queen of angels, of the
new creation, and of humanity. Mary lifts them up. "Come, let

us adore Christ. He went into Heaven. He prepared an eternal dwelling for His Mother."[152]

Then thousands of celebrating angels sang sublime melodies. They were the most beautiful harmonies that had ever been heard resonating under the vault of Heaven. The assembly of the firstborn whose names are inscribed in Heaven advanced amid cries of joy. They were dressed in white and were glowing and affected by love. Their wounds, imperfections, illnesses, and handicap were transcended and dressed in light. These told their story. All of them were going toward Christ, the Mediator of the New Covenant, who saved them by His blood and reconciled them to His Father. The Father took each one of His children in His arms. He consoled them and wiped away their flowing tears. "It's over, my little one, my beautiful one, my love. It's over. You are forever saved and safe and secure." The most bountiful earthly feasts are a pale reflection of this assembly's magnificence. The purest earthly joys are nothing compared with the infinite happiness that took hold of everyone at this sight.

O Lord, God of love, we want to stay beside You forever, and rejoice and contemplate You with Jesus and Mary, the beautiful angels, all the those we have loved and cherished on earth, the saints we have prayed to, the people we have helped, all disciples of the same God, and all children of the same Father, in the eternal joy that will never be taken away from us (see Heb. 12:22–24; Rev. 21).

---

[152] André Gouzes invitatory "Venez adorons le Christ" [Come, let us adore Christ] from *Liturgie chorale du peuple de Dieu: Vêpres de l'Assomption de la Vierge Marie* [Choral liturgy from the people of God: vespers of the Assumption of the Virgin Mary].

The Hope of Heaven

Mary's Assumption into Heaven started with her saying yes in Nazareth. Each yes to God is a step toward Heaven and eternal life. For the Lord wants us all to be with Him in His home![153]

Angels surrounded their sovereign and protégée. She was finally here! St. John of Damascus thought that Mary's body was carried to the Garden of Gethsemane by the apostles and was "preceded and followed by a procession of angels, who covered her with their wings," as in the past with the Ark of the Covenant.

"In Mary, indeed," said Pope Benedict XVI, "we contemplate that reality of glory to which each one of us and the entire Church is called."[154] Mary's *fiat* (her yes) echoed the dawn of the ages in the *non serviam* (I will not serve) of Lucifer and his angels: Yes, Lord, I really want to do Your will. For Your will is sweet. It is my joy and strength. I want to participate in humanity's plan of salvation, for it is a happy plan.

The Angel Led Catherine to Mary

On the night of July 18–19, 1830, at 140 rue du Bac in Paris, in the Sisters of Charity convent, St. Catherine Labouré was awakened by a light that was illuminating her cell and by a small hand that was gently shaking her. A beautiful child was standing near her bed. He appeared to be four or five years old and was completely dressed in white. Rays of light emerged from him and lit up the room. Catherine wondered: "How did he get in?"

---

[153] Francis, tweet, August 15, 2019.
[154] Benedict XVI, Angelus, August 15, 2012.

"Sister," he said, "everybody is sound asleep. Come to the chapel. The Virgin Mary is waiting for you."

Catherine did not know if she was dreaming or if all this was real. But she obeyed; she quickly got out of her bed and put her clothes on. She followed the child, who brightened the dark hallways with his presence. He led her to the chapel. There, she said, she heard the "rustling of a silk dress." She saw a lady sitting in the choir near the altar, in the chair where the priest normally sat. The child said to Catherine: "Here is the Virgin Mary."

The young nun did not move. She was astonished. The child repeated this a little louder: "Here is the Virgin Mary."

Then Catherine hurried toward her Heavenly Mother. Falling to her knees, she put her hands on Mary's lap. Mary gently spoke to her and gave her advice for her prayer life. What an extraordinary moment! Catherine later confided that it was "the sweetest moment of her life."

The Virgin Mary spoke to her for two hours and entrusted her with the mission of having what we today call the Miraculous Medal made and promoted. Then the Virgin Mary went away. Catherine had the impression that every light was turned off all at once. The only thing that remained was the soft glow of the little angel, who led her back to her cell.

We can read this prayer to the Queen of Angels in Our Lady of the Angels Basilica. She is tenderly and compassionately leaning toward each one of us:

O Lady of the Angels, obtain for us, through the intercession of blessed Francis, pardon for our sins; help us to keep away from sin and indifference, so that we shall be worthy of calling you our Mother for evermore. Bless our

homes, our toil, and our rest, by giving us that same serenity
we experience within the walls of the Portiuncula, where
hate, guilt, and tears turn into a song of joy like that once
sung by the angels and the seraphic Francis. Help those who
are in need and hungry, those who are in danger of body and
soul, those who are sad and downhearted, those who are
sick and dying. Bless us, your most beloved children, and
we pray you, bless also with the same motherly gesture, all
those who are innocent, together with those who are guilty;
those who are faithful, together with those who have gone
astray; those who believe, together with those who are in
doubt. Bless all humanity, so that all men acknowledging
that they are God's children, would find through love, real
peace and real good. Amen

Fr. Lamy tells us:

Angels surrounded her with such simplicity and affection!
God has given her thousands and thousands of them. She
knows them all by name. They know her only by one
name: Queen.

Father Boudon, in his introduction to the treatise *La dévo-
tion aux neuf choeurs des Saints Anges* (The devotion to the nine
choirs of the holy angels) writes:

Prostrated at your feet, O my powerful protector, I offer
and you and dedicate this little work to you in honor of
all of the nine choirs of angels, your faithful subjects, and
the illustrious princes of your divine court. As you are
their lovely Princess, their imposing Empress, and their
glorious Lady, it is only fair that I dedicate what is in their
best interest and what affects their glory.

Encounters with Angels

Mary and the End Times

St. Louis-Marie Grignion de Montfort and Marthe Robin, who were separated by two centuries, both prophesied about the end times by announcing that Jesus would return in the same way He had come — through Mary! Each time we recite a Hail Mary, with the words of the angel Gabriel, we hasten the coming of Jesus in His glory and in our lives.

In the third secret of Fatima, which Sr. Lucia gave to the Vatican in 1944 and was made public on June 26, 2000, we see the Virgin Mary protecting humanity:

At the left of Our Lady and a little above, we saw an Angel with a flaming sword in his left hand; flashing it gave out flames that looked as though they would set the world on fire; but they died out in contact with the splendor that Our Lady radiated toward him from her right hand.[155]

We can have recourse to her in our great trials as well as our little sorrows, for she understands and perceives everything and rocks us in her lap, as Fr. Louis-Édouard Cestac tell us:

O good Mother, O sweet Mother, Immaculate Spouse of Heaven and Queen of the blessed spirits who contemplate Him with you in Heaven, you are and will always be our love, hope, help, and refuge.

"Our Home Is in Heaven"

The saints have so longed for the next life that they remind us that we are only passing through life on this earth. Mother

---

[155] Congregation for the Doctrine of Faith, "The Message of Fatima," Vatican website.

Yvonne-Aimée de Malestroit said it well. She benefited from her guardian angel's very attentive help to the point where she felt like him:

> It seems that God first wanted to create me for Heaven. Then, changing His mind, He dropped me on the earth. The angel gave me this mysterious life of love, this insight into people and things, and these extraordinary abilities that the most educated men will never understand.

In His love, God gives us time to be fulfilled and reach our potential before being led to the perfect world where we will no longer change, grow older, or deteriorate, and where we will no longer be able to grow in holiness. *Come as you are!* Yes, we will be taken as we are.

So, let us take advantage of the time that is given us to grow even more! May we listen better, pay more attention to others, and grow in love.

> My child, become Love. No one on this earth can prevent you from becoming what you were created to be, unless you give someone this power by listening to him instead of Me. I love you tenderly.[156]

It is never easy to dive into the unknown. Is there a greater chasm than the one between this life and the next? Jesus Himself was afraid of it. But let us not fear this gate on the brink of

---

[156] Léandre Lachance, *Pour le bonheur des Miens, Mes choisis — Jésus* [For the happiness of my loved ones, my chosen ones — Jesus], vol. 1, no. 77. Each morning, we can receive a thought for the day by registering on the website of the Foundation of the Chosen Ones of Jesus, www.fdcj.org

which our earthly mother and our Heavenly Mother are waiting for us with a smile!

Prayer

St. Michael, prince of the heavenly host, I beseech you to answer me. I beg you to take my soul into your most holy custody on the last day and to lead it to the place of refreshment, peace, and rest, where the souls of the saints wait with inexpressible joy for the upcoming judgment and glorious resurrection. Whether I am speaking or silent, watching, walking, or resting, help me to continue accomplishing my works in all that I do. Protect me from demons' temptations and the pains of Hell. Amen.[157]

---

[157] Based on a fifteenth-century manuscript.

Conclusion

I will finish with a personal testimony. In July 2015, my husband and I were on the GR, a long-distance hiking trail that extends two hundred kilometers over the main hilltops in Corsica. It is considered to be one of the most difficult trails in Europe. On that day, the hike was especially long and rough. We were on the Aiguilles de Bavella. To make the walk more rhythmic, I recited very simple prayers in my head. I also sang calm, meditative songs on the slopes and dynamic ones where it wasn't as steep. On a really steep slope, when we were going rather quickly (for the restaurant on the slope was calling out to us — a true restaurant after six days in a mountain refuge!), I started to sing to the angels in my head (see the prayer below).

Shortly afterward, my left foot slid or bumped into my stick. Down I went, head first, onto the rocky path. I injured my legs on the first landing. As in a slow-motion film, I saw the second landing, where my head was about to crash against a block of stone.

That is when I felt a very gentle hand on my cheek. Then my head hit the stone. I was aware of the anxiety of my husband, who was following me and reached me in one leap. I was completely clear-headed and cried out: "It's okay, it's okay, I'm fine!"

Encounters with Angels

Blood was flowing profusely from the top of my head into my hands. But my husband examined me and saw that it was not a serious wound. The pressure of a handkerchief quickly stopped the bleeding. In spite of the wounds in my tibias and my head, everything was fine! I could have had a much more serious fall or even broken my glasses, a finger, or a tooth—which would have meant the end of our journey.

I will never forget the gentleness of that hand on my cheek. As we come to the end of this little trip that we have been on together, I hope you will experience it too.

We met many very different angels. But they were all magnificent, devoted, and admirable. They wanted us to know the mysteries of Heaven, like a traveler from a sunny country who wants his hosts to discover its light and warmth.

After this reading, will you feel like living more in the presence of the angels who surround us, requesting their advice, asking for their help, and placing yourself under their protection? Will you more often think about thanking them and praying to them, experiencing the Mass in their company, and letting yourself be guided by them to become more intimate with God?

Here is a prayer that you can sing or recite before a trip or for a problem or worry that a family member has:

Prayer

O Commanders of the heavenly hosts,
We the unworthy beseech you, through
your entreaties you will fortify us,
Guarding us in the shelter of the wings of your
ethereal glory,

Conclusion

Even as we fervently bow before You, crying:
Deliver us from all danger as commanders
of the powers on high.[158]

I will end with this prayer that my grandmother gave me:

Good evening, my good angel,
I commend myself to God and to you.
You have watched over me during the day.
Watch over me tonight,
Easily and safely,
And without offending you or my God.
I surrender my soul to God
Today and throughout my life.
Amen.

---

[158] Troparion to St. Michael the Archangel.

Appendix

Some Theological Clarifications

I invite you to read this appendix, which will not exhaust the subject of angels, but will clarify it a little, while listening to Allegri's *Miserere*.

Who Are the Angels?

"By faith we understand that the world was created by the word of God" (Heb. 11:3).

It is not easy to talk about angels: "What will I say about angelic spirits? I am only an earthworm."[159] Nevertheless, keeping everything in proportion, it is good for believers to be acquainted with some very basic ideas on "the invisible world" that we cite in the Creed. A certain prevailing angelology and some popular series are spreading a vision of angels, demons, and even God that have nothing to do with what the Church teaches. Let us discover the real angels, not those of reality TV!

In fact, when the Scriptures use the expression "heaven and earth," "heaven" refers to "the spiritual creatures, the angels, who surround God" (CCC 326). The word "angel," in Latin (*angelus*), Hebrew (*malakh*), and Greek (*aggelos*), means "messenger": "Angels are spiritual creatures who glorify God without

---

[159] St. Bernard of Clairvaux.

ceasing and who serve his saving plans for other creatures" (CCC 350). Believing in angels is neither optional nor folkloric. The existence of the angels is "a truth of faith" (CCC 328).

The angel is a pure spirit. He is not subject to the same rules of space and time as we are. The angel is not eternal because he has a beginning, but he is incorruptible and immortal because he does not have a body. His understanding is keener than ours, and his will is firmer.

According to St. Augustine: "'Angel' is the name of their office, not of their nature. If you seek the name of their nature, it is 'spirit'; if you seek the name of their office, it is 'angel': from what they are, 'spirit', from what they do, 'angel.'"[160]

Clothed with light and glowing with charity, angels talk to us about God's glory and beauty. They are the living reflections of the face they contemplate.

Their number is fixed because they cannot reproduce. They were created by God one by one, once and for all, when the world started. "Then I looked, and I heard around the throne and the living creatures and the elders the voice of many angels, numbering myriads of myriads and thousands of thousands" (Rev. 5:11). The angel's nature is not the same as man's. One will never become the other:

We often hear about a child who had died: "He has become an angel." No! He is in glory and in the light among the saints and angels to sing the praise and glory of the Lord in full voice. But He does not add another angel to the heavenly legions! They have a different nature and are called to different purposes in the order of

---

[160] St. Augustine, *En. in Ps.* 103, 1, 15: *PL* 37, 1348, quoted in CCC 329.

Creation—in God's plan. Angels are an integral part of the organization of the cosmos, as God intended.[161]

The Nine Choirs of Angels

St. Thomas Aquinas, "the Angelic Doctor" (1225–1274), established a hierarchy of nine classes of angels from a synthesis that starts with the Old Testament, St. Paul, the Church Fathers (especially St. Gregory the Great), and Pseudo-Dionysius:[162]

First degree, the celestial court:

1. The seraphim "are fiery and eager beings who burn with God's love."[163]
2. The mission of the cherubim is "to pray and bless" and to know God.
3. Thrones are "bearers of God and seats of God" and "the foundations of the world. They represent God's justice and authority."[164]

Second degree, the government of the world:

1. Dominions "pass God's will on to other angels."
2. Virtues "carry out divine wishes."
3. Powers "fight against God's enemy."

Third degree, assistance to humanity:

1. Principalities "govern and protect the country."
2. Archangels "govern human communities, announce important events, and protect the Church. According

---

[161] Nicole Timbal, *Les Anges, messagers de lumière* [Angels, messengers of light] (Paris: EdB, 2011).

[162] Thomas Aquinas, *Summa Theologica*, I, q. 108.

[163] Thanks to my marvelous friend Martine Bazin, who let me use here the explanations in her book *Saint Michel, protégez la France* [St. Michael, protect France] (Paris: Éditions Pierre Téqui, 2017).

[164] St. Thomas Aquinas.

to the Old Testament, there are seven of them.[165] But
the Catholic Church names only St. Michael, St.
Raphael, and St. Gabriel.
3. Angels "personally guide and accompany each soul."
The prophet Isaiah and St. Teresa of Ávila each met a seraph,
as we have previously seen. St. Angela of Foligno told us about
the dazzling thrones:

I saw Jesus Christ arriving with an army of Angels, and
the magnificence of His escort was savored by my soul
with immense pleasure. I was surprised I was able to rejoice at the sight of the Angels, because, as a rule, all my
joy is focused on Jesus Christ. But I soon noticed in my
soul two perfectly distinct joys: one coming from God,
the other from the Angels. But they did not resemble
each other. I was admiring the magnificence which surrounded the Lord. I asked what it was that I was witness-
ing. "They are the Thrones," a voice said. The multitude
was dazzling and infinite, so much so that, if number and
measure were not laws of creation, I would have thought
that the sublime crowd before my eyes was countless and
boundless.[166]

---

[165] Tob. 12:15: "I am Raphael, one of the seven angels who stand
ready and enter before the glory of the Lord."
[166] Angela of Foligno, *The Book of Visions*, chap. 37, quoted in
"Blessed Angela of Foligno," Real Presence Association, http://
www.therealpresence.org/eucharst/misc/Angels_Demons/AN-
GES_foligno.pdf.

Their Mission

Their mission is on three levels:

1 In God's service: "With their whole being the angels are *servants* and messengers of God" (CCC 329). They stand in His presence day and night to contemplate, praise, and serve Him.

2. In the service of the Church: "The whole life of the Church benefits from the mysterious and powerful help of angels," especially in celebration and praise: "In her liturgy, the Church joins with the angels to adore the thrice-holy God" (CCC 334, 335).

3. In our service: "From its beginning until death, human life is surrounded by their watchful care and inter-cession." Angels and human beings share the same destiny, which is to be united with God in eternal happiness. But the angel is already there, whereas mankind is still on the way: "Man and, through him all creation, is destined for the glory of God" (CCC 336, 353).

Here are three assumptions that need to be intertwined:

1. Angels can act with their own will.

2. Angels always act with and for love.

3. Angels always do everything in compliance with God's will.

The result, therefore, is magnificent. These extraordinary beings, who are almost perfect, who master space and matter, and who radiate love in each of their gestures and words, are here to help us!

Imagine that you are climbing Mont Blanc. It is difficult. You are a little worried. Then, suddenly, the best Chamonix guides show up next to you! It's not just one guide who calls from the summit: "You're almost there!" All the guides who have ever existed and will exist in these beautiful mountains are near you and following in your footsteps. They guide and advise you at each moment. This will not, of course, give you the physical condition that you are lacking ("I should not have skipped my gym classes"). But if you listen to their wise recommendations, your progress will be impressive.

Guardian Angels, a Unique Gift

St. Basil told us that "beside each believer stands an angel as protector and shepherd leading him to life."[167] St. Thomas said: "Each man has an angel guardian appointed to him."[168]

"Wait," you will tell me, "don't we already have our patron saints and all the saints who intercede for us, especially those with whom we are maintaining a privileged relationship; deceased members of our families whose edifying lives have left their mark on us and who are praying for us; Mary, our sweet Mother, whose loving presence surrounds us; and, above all, God, who is three Persons in one—the Holy Trinity, from whom all love comes? It includes the Father, who gives us life, the Son, who gives us salvation, and the Holy Spirit, who gives us His gifts and fruits."

Yes, of course! Let us never forget that all our prayers, requests, and praises, whether they go through a saint, a priest, a friend, or a guardian angel, are for God. For all comes from Him and goes back to Him. Yet, at certain times, we need the power of the Holy Spirit. At other times, we need to pray to

[167] St. Basil, *Adv. Eunomium* III, I: PG 29,656B, quoted in CCC 336.
[168] Thomas Aquinas, *Summa Theologica*, I, q. 113, art. 2.

St. Joseph. At still other times, only the presence of Jesus by our side satisfies us.

We see the overabundance of His love in creation. God loves life. He creates thousands of wildflowers, thousands of stars in the cosmos, and thousands of angels. We love to be *favorites*. It's in our human nature. This is why God's unique gift of an angel *for ourselves alone* is so precious!

For each of us, the guardian angel is an unparalleled and marvelous gift that God offers us from our conception to our death. For our angel's mission will end there, but not his affection for us! We will no longer need his help. But we will continue to appreciate his familiar presence. So many billions of human beings since the dawn of time to the end of the world! So many guardian angels to watch over them in unique and personal ways!

They are the lowest of all the angels in the hierarchy. But that does not mean that they are less important or glorious than the highest angels. Jesus tells us: "See that you do not despise one of these little ones; for I tell you that in heaven their angels always behold the face of my Father who is in heaven" (Matt. 18:10). Angels see God. They hope that we will experience this great joy. They will do all that they can to lead us to it.

Invocation Prayer to the Nine Choirs of Angels

*Most ardent seraphim, make me burn with the love of the
 thrice-holy God!*

*Radiant cherubim, grant me the understanding of the things
 above!*

Admirable thrones, give me peace of soul!

*Sovereign dominions, help me be victorious over every bad
 tendency.*

Encounters with Angels

Invincible virtues, enable me to be strong against evil spirits.
Serene principalities, assist me in controlling my passions!
Heavenly powers, help me conform to God's will!
Victorious archangels, help me to walk confidently in God's
ways!
Blessed angels, enable me to be unfailingly faithful and
deeply humble!
O choirs of heavenly angels, make it possible for me to sing
with you with my mouth and my heart, throughout my
life, starting here on earth and for all eternity: Holy!
Holy! Holy is the Lord, God of hosts! Heaven and earth
are filled with the majesty of Your glory! Amen.

"Oh, the Beautiful Angel!"

St. Thomas Aquinas declared that "angels need an assumed body, not for themselves, but on our account."[169] The Bible gives them various accessories—wings, long white robes, and luminous clothes. But they are not dependent on this material. They can look like a butterfly, a dove, a lamb, a young child, a teenager, or a strong man.

Beauty is what they have in common. Writings such as the testimony of the saints tell us that angels are very beautiful and covered with light. When they communicate with men, angels usually take on human forms, but without shining or showing something about their excellent nature in the material they use. It doesn't matter whether it's in an imaginary or a fleetingly real way. This is why they invariably have a youthful appearance and are surrounded by light with magnificent features. Giovanni P. Siena, an Italian writer, who was Padre Pio's friend for more

---

[169] Thomas Aquinas, *Summa Theologica*, I, q. 51, art. 2.

than thirty years, tells us that "they give the impression of being exceptionally prestigious and strong."[170]

Fr. Lamy saw his angel with wavy black hair, whereas St. Frances of Rome's angel had long blond curls. Marie de Sainte-Cécile de Rome said: "How beautiful my guardian angel is!"

The angel Gabriel appeared next to the Virgin Mary on the Île-Bouchard in 1947. "He was wearing a white robe. His hand was resting on his chest. Jacqueline Aubry, one of the little seers, said that his hair was white and shaped the way English women would wear it." Jeannette, the youngest seer, who was only seven, cried out: "Oh, the beautiful angel! Oh, the beautiful angel!"

Catherine of Genoa thought that, in angels, beauty was combined with joy: "Angels? Their beautiful, joyous faces with eyes so simple, pure, and clear—I could not help laughing."

When Joan of Arc's judges asked her what St. Michael looked like, she retorted with her usual outspokenness:

"I didn't see him wearing a crown. As for his clothes, I don't know."

"Was he naked?"

"Do you think our Lord has nothing to clothe him with?"

"Did he have hair?"

"And why would they have cut it?"

Beauty, a Gift of God

A mother testified after her baby's death: "Beauty is a gift of God to reduce my suffering." But, you say, we talk about "the devil's beauty." The devil is beautiful or, in any case, makes us think that he is in order to seduce us. Jesus, on the other hand, even

---

[170] Giovanni Siena, *Padre Pio "Voici l'heure des anges"* [This is the time for angels] (Paris: Éditions Pierre Téqui, 2015).

though He was called "the most handsome of men" (see Ps. 45:2), was disfigured in His Passion and "had no form or comeliness that we should look at him, and no beauty that we should desire him" (Isa. 53:2).

In his film *La Beauté du Diable*[171] (Beauty and the devil), René Clair revisits the myth of Faust and gives Gérard Philippe's handsome face to the impertinent devil, who promises to give the elderly Faust youth and beauty in exchange for his soul. René Clair's quest for eternal youth had only just begun, with the specter of nuclear weapons. He was going to be the first filmmaker to join the French Academy in 1960:

> The character that is Faust strangely illuminates the light of our time. The great intellectual current that impelled alchemists to research the philosopher's stone and the secrets of matter continued until the age of atomic discoveries. Our contemporaries are privileged to witness the strange spectacle of a humanity that, having sold its soul to science, is trying to prevent the damnation of the world toward which its own works are leading it.

As the critic Antoine Royer stresses:

> The beautiful, great, and magnificent idea of the film, therefore, is this transfer of characters and reversal of roles that sees an insolent young devil invite a bedridden bearded man to become as beautiful as he is."[172]

Saints have asked themselves how we distinguish a heavenly apparition from a demonic visit. Because the devil is also the

---

[171] 1950 French-Italian film.
[172] September 1, 2011, chronicle on DVDClassik.com.

father of lies, he often dresses in light to attract us. Evil can hide under the appearance of goodness. This discernment, which is the whole issue of Original Sin, is not easy. God said to man: "Of the tree of the knowledge of good and evil you shall not eat" (Gen. 2:17). Saints often rely on their spiritual directors to decide if such-and-such an apparition or such-and-such a revelation comes from God.

Jesus Himself gave this criterion to Catherine of Siena: The devil's visit provides some pleasure at first; then the individual feels annoyed, disgusted, and proud. On the contrary, an angel's visit starts by inspiring fear; then the individual feels comforted and surrounded by gentleness.

When she was afraid of being visited by a demon, Agnes of Langeac was ordered by her confessor to kick her guardian angel when he showed up. She hesitated, torn between her desire to obey and the great respect she felt for this young man whose presence was so familiar. Her confessor, knowing the cause of her distress, gently made fun of her and advised her to be obedient. She complied by gently pushing him with the tip of her foot. He congratulated her for her obedience.

What Is Beauty?

"Did you know that you have beautiful eyes?" Do young generations still know this famous line from Jean Gabin in *Le Quai des brumes* (Port of shadows)?[173] The question bothered me when, by accident, I saw a picture of the scene. Above all, would our teenagers find this Michèle Morgan beautiful? She no longer conforms to ideals of contemporary beauty. Her hair was too short and too flat on top with curls that were excessively rigid.

---

[173] 1938 Marcel Carné French film.

Encounters with Angels

Her upper lip was too thin, and her heart-shaped mouth was too pronounced. But her eyes (and their pure, transparent blue look) still touch me because of their beauty.

Beauty is ephemeral, not only because it fades but also because the codes that one generation has enacted to define beauty will be considered out of date by the following generation. Then they will end up coming back because fashion is cyclical. Beauty can also seem subjective. We all have our own criteria. Such-and-such a manly actor pleases some, whereas he repels others. This is even truer of works of art. Suddenly, without our knowing why, a face or a piece of music will be exciting and will travel around the world. It will be universally popular—i.e., one soul and one soul-to-soul encounter that is beyond fads and words. It is in a pure perception that speaks to us about another beauty, which is a timeless one. We have its memory and desire. St. Augustine said that "if we knew the beauty of angels, we would be amazed by it." This amazement, whose trace we have kept in what spiritual authors call "the cutting edge of the soul," is this untouched space where God has inalterably left His mark.

When art is inspired—and it can be inspired in many ways, even escaping the artist's mastery—it is a bridge between the invisible world and our earthly existence. It is the promise that this yearning that we bear for what is beautiful is meaningful. It will be satisfied someday when we will see Him as He is. He is the Author of all beauty and the one whose gaze we met before we were born and that we were desperately looking for. "Late have I loved you, Beauty so ancient and so new, late have I loved you! Lo, you were within, but I outside.... You were with me, but I was not with you.[174]

[174] St. Augustine, *Conf.* 3, 6, 11.

Meditation

You were the signet of perfection, full of wisdom and perfect in beauty. You were in Eden, the garden of God; every precious stone was your covering, carnelian, chryso-lite, and moonstone, beryl, onyx, and jasper, sapphire, turquoise, and emerald; and worked in gold were your settings and your engravings. On the day that you were created they were prepared. (Ezek. 28:12–13)

The Fall Will Be Harder

When He said: "So the last will be first" (Matt. 20:16), Jesus was not thinking about Lucifer, the most brilliant angel. He was the one who bore light and the first creature with whom God wanted to share His love and power. But he turned away from God by wanting only power and not love.

A Free Choice

Angels were subject, like men after them, to the test of freedom. They had to choose before seeing God face-to-face. Lucifer preferred to go far away from God out of pride because he wanted to be like God on his own. He did not want to receive this likeness from God:

He desired resemblance with God in this respect — by desiring, as his last end of beatitude, something which he could attain by the virtue of his own nature, turning his appetite away from supernatural beatitude, which is attained by God's grace. Or, if he desired as his last end that likeness of God which is bestowed by grace, he sought to have it by the power of his own nature.[175]

---

[175] Thomas Aquinas, *Summa Theologica*, I, q. 63, art. 3.

Encounters with Angels

There is no question that these angels would place themselves in the service of men, these imperfect, fragile, fickle creatures who are limited in time and space! Lucifer (the bearer of light), who became Satan ("the accuser" and "the adversary") or the devil ("the one who divides" and "the one who deceives"), would, on the contrary, work on making these poor human beings, who were cherished by God, his slaves. He would do this in order to trample on love, mercy, compassion, and tenderness—i.e., all he detests for having refused it.

> War arose in heaven, Michael and his angels fighting against the dragon; and the dragon and his angels fought, but they were defeated and there was no longer any place for them in heaven. And the great dragon was thrown down, that ancient serpent, who is called the Devil and Satan, the deceiver of the whole world—he was thrown down to the earth, and his angels were thrown down with him. (Rev. 12:7–9)

Most spiritual authors (but not St. Thomas Aquinas!) think that Satan was in the highest level of the angelic hierarchy. He was a seraph. But according to Fr. Rémi Griveau, the pastor of Saint-Germain de Charonne in Paris, Lucifer was a cherub. His mission was to know God. Knowledge can lead to pride, whereas pure love always leads to goodness.

An Irreversible Choice

The angels' free and voluntary choice was also a final choice: "The angel's will adheres fixedly and immovably."[176] It was no longer possible for the angels who remained faithful to God to

---

[176] Thomas Aquinas, *Summa Theologica*, I, q. 64, art. 2.

fall, and Satan and his accomplices could no longer be saved. From now on, the spiritual struggle would be played out in every moment of world history up to the final return of Jesus in His glory. At that time, the judgment of all souls will be surrendered into the Father's hands.

We must imagine in what a dilemma these marvelous creatures, who were more perfect than we are, found themselves. They put the love of God, their Creator, below themselves, while they were so close to it. God placed death and life, unhappiness and joy before them. Lucifer responded: "*Non serviam.* I will not serve You." He did not, in fact, want to be addicted to love by receiving God in His beauty, intelligence, and greatness. He turned away from God to focus on himself, says St. Augustine: "The holy angels, who turned toward the Word, became light. The bad angels, who dwelled within themselves, turned into night."

Having inescapably created their own misfortune, they now look for only one thing: they desire to attract the most human beings, like the dunce who wants to divert the good students from the teacher's lesson in order to feel less lonely in his foolishness. For we are really foolish! How many times do we choose the wide path of destruction because "everyone is doing it" whereas the narrow path of salvation, with its charm, is steep and stony. But how rewarding it is to contemplate the open skies when we reach the top!

Hell is not an exterior punishment that is inflicted by God. It is the state of a heart that has completely collapsed on itself and is entirely alone. It has fallen into the chasm of self-justification by refusing to receive grace. God does not condemn anyone. We are the ones who condemn ourselves. Divine mercy is infinite. But it can do nothing for the one who refuses it. This refusal is the sin against the Holy Spirit.[177]

Why Must We Believe in Angels?

"We can hardly guess what is on earth, and what is at hand we find with labor" (Wisd. 9:16). Can't we be satisfied with some simple truth without having to add complex notions like the mystery of the Trinity or the nature of angels? We already have enough work taking care of the worries that clutter "our minds with a thousand thoughts."

The response is given to us in the continuation of the text from the book of Wisdom: "Who has learned thy counsel, unless thou hast given wisdom and sent thy holy Spirit from on high? And thus the paths of those on earth were set right" (Wisd. 9:17–18). Angels take hold of all the graces that the Holy Spirit gives and distributes them to mankind. They put God's will within our reach. They guide us by walking the path with us. Demons do the same thing, but the other way around. They are always by us to throw us off balance and make us fall and lose ourselves. When we turn our backs on love, they win a victory. When we perform an act of love, it is the angels who rejoice and goodness that moves in and around us. All that we say or do influences our environment. Why are the surroundings of monasteries so beautiful? It is, of course, because monks cultivate and maintain the soil out of respect for nature, but it is also because their prayers and chants create a spiritual climate that benefits all of nature. One day, a Desert Father

---

[177] Charles Becquérieux, "Pécher contre l'Esprit?" [To sin against the Spirit?], *France Catholique*, no. 3636, June 7, 2016, 26.

received a vision of a big city on which an indifferent demon reigned supreme, whereas, a little farther away, legions of demons raged in a perpetual mass movement on top of a tiny convent.

Each of our lives and each of our souls entails, at times, struggles between angels and demons, between good and evil. Angels, who have made the right choice and rejoice about it at every moment, hope we also will make that good choice. They help us with all their strength and love.

Prayer

How you are fallen from heaven,
O Day Star, son of Dawn!
How you are cut down to the ground,
you who laid the nations low!
You said in your heart,
"I will ascend to heaven;
above the stars of God
I will set my throne on high;
I will sit on the mount of assembly
in the far north;
I will ascend above the heights of the clouds,
I will make myself like the Most High."
But you are brought down to Sheol,
to the depths of the Pit. (Isa. 14:12–15)

Angels in Art

In Rembrandt's *Ascension of* Christ (1636), aren't the six chubby little angels with the colorful wings adorable? They are lifting the cloud on which Jesus is standing to carry Him up to Heaven. We find so many angels in artistic depictions, but they are hardly present in our prayer lives. What a paradox!

Encounters with Angels

Painters and sculptors have always been inspired by the supernatural dimension of these creatures. Since there are so few details in the biblical texts on their physical aspect, artists have enjoyed total freedom. From Fra Angelico to Chagall, and including Raphael,[178] Titian, Caravaggio, Rubens, Rembrandt, Poussin, Gauguin, and Van Gogh, they competed with their talents to express the magnificence of these creatures, who come from Paradise but work on earth.[179]

Three Examples among Hundreds

Let us look at *The Dream of the Magi*, a scene that was sculpted by Gislebertus on a column in the Autun Cathedral between 1120 and 1125. The magi, who were guided by the star, discovered the Child Jesus with Mary, His Mother. Then, after bowing down before Him and offering Him their gifts, they went to sleep, exhausted by their long trip. An angel appeared to them in a dream to warn them not to return to Herod, who wanted to kill the Child:

The eyes of one of the three kings were opened. He was just awakened by the angel, who touched his pinkie with his finger. The messenger's wings spread out. He showed him the star that guided them toward the Messiah. The star could be taken for an eight-petaled flower. These wise men, who came from the East, let themselves be guided.[180]

---

[178] Let us think about the amusing composition of Raphael's painting *The Sistine Madonna*, where both cherubim or *putti* are leaning on the bottom frame with their arms.

[179] Michael Lonsdale, *Sur les ailes de la beauté* [On the wings of beauty] (Paris: Éditions Philippe Rey, 2018).

[180] Sophie Roubertie, Instagram publication on August 10, 2019.

Another sculpture, which dates back to 1240, is the *Smiling Angel*,[181] a statue at the northern entrance of the Reims Cathedral, "the Cathedral of the Angels":

> We cannot do without the Reims angel, which is the most famous angel in France. He is calm, elegant, and leaning against a column — the *Smiling Angel*. Curiously, he is questioning me. What is this mysterious smile hiding? Is it goodness or kindness? Or is it a sly smile or a provocative nothing? Is it the angel of the Annunciation, who is expressing inner joy, peace, trust, and the spiritual drive and full awareness of his role? I do not know.... There is something in his smile that is reserved and mysterious.[182]

Let us not forget the icon of *The Trinity* by Andre Rublev (1410–1427), whose spiritual theme is the Holy Trinity but which literally represents Abraham's hospitality — that is to say, the arrival of the three angels at the oak of Mamre:

> Three angels, who were recognizable because of their wings, were seated around a table.... They (these three people) were ageless. Yet they seemed young. They did not have a gender. Nonetheless, they were steady and graceful.... Each of the three angels was carrying a very thin, elongated stick. Each divine person was a traveler and a pilgrim.... The three sticks formed a declaration and a promise, which declared that the three had already

---

[181] I have entrusted to this angel everyone who reads this book, as I had just finished writing it and was in Reims for the feast of Christ the King.

[182] Nicole Timbal, *Les Anges*.

come to men. They promised that the three would come again. Our God in three Persons comes forever.[183]

The Mission of Art

The pianist and jazz composer Bill Evans declared this in 1959: "My idea of art is that it must enhance the human being. It is a sort of lesson about spirituality to show a part of oneself that could not have been discovered otherwise. For it is relatively easy to rediscover oneself in part. But only art can let us be aware of this secret part that has been hidden from ourselves up to this point. Art's real mission is for the artist to be able to find this universal dimension in himself and to express it in terms that are intelligible to the common man."[184]

Angels often intervene in the Bible, the history of the Church, and the history of men. Theology teaches us that they are pure, nonmaterial spirits. But knowledge goes through our senses. Men frequently need to see in order to understand. So artists very willingly take hold of these episodes, which are often quite striking, to make them visible to us and, therefore, more easily understood. It is true that an Annunciation is immediately more accessible to our understanding with an angel that is present than without one.

Angels offer artists another advantage. Since they are not endowed with a physical body, the artist enjoys complete freedom to represent them. They can be with or

[183] Commentary of Fr. Lev Gillet, a monk of the Eastern church.
[184] Quoted by Patrice Blanc-Francard, "Bill Evans," *Dictionnaire amoureux du jazz* [Jazz lover's dictionary] (Paris: Plon, 2018), 239.

without wings, and with colorful or white wings. They can be sensitive musical angels or powerful angels who conquer demons. They can be in armor or in fine tunics....

Perhaps we are less sensitive to the supernatural in our rather rational times. But for several centuries, the eruption of the divine in human lives may not have seemed so extraordinary. Since the existence of God and angels was generally accepted, their frequent representation was not at all astonishing.[185]

The Church tells us that

> *sacred art* is true and beautiful when its form corresponds to its particular vocation: evoking and glorifying, in faith and adoration, the transcendent mystery of God—the surpassing invisible beauty of truth and love visible in Christ.... This spiritual beauty of God is reflected in the most holy Virgin Mother of God, the angels, and saints. Genuine sacred art draws men to adoration, to prayer, and to the love of God, Creator and Savior, the Holy One and Sanctifier. (CCC 2502)

Angels and the Greatest Love

When the Risen Jesus appeared to His apostles, He showed Thomas the marks of His Passion: "Put your finger here, and see my hands; and put out your hand, and place it in my side; do

---

[185] Author's conversation with Sophie Roubertie, who is in charge of the newspaper column "Apprendre à voir" [Learn to see] for *ActuAiles*, a bimonthly news magazine for ten- to fifteen-year-old children (actuailes.fr). Roubertie is also the author of the book *Apprendre à voir—La vie dans l'art* [Learn to see—life in art] (Paris: Éditions Téqui, 2018).

not be faithless, but believing" (John 20:27). Some saints later received these marks, which are called stigmata and are as painful as they are glorious. They are a proof of love and of the salvation that were obtained at the price of blood.

> Christ knew why He kept the scars in His body. For, as He showed them to Thomas who would not believe except he handled and saw them, so will He show His wounds to His enemies, so that He who is the Truth may convict them, saying: "Behold the man whom you crucified; see the wounds you inflicted; recognize the side you pierced, since it was opened by you and for you, yet you would not enter."[186]

On September 17, 1224, two years before his death, St. Francis of Assisi asked for the grace to understand the immense love that Christ bore during His Passion. The response was astonishing:

> While he was very meditatively contemplating the Savior's suffering, Francis saw a seraph come down from Heaven. He looked like a crucified man who was attached to a cross. This heavenly spirit had six wings of fire. Two of them rose above his head, whereas the other two spread out to fly. The last two covered his whole body. Francis' soul was joyful and sad before this strange sight. The seraph approached him. Five rays of light and fire sprang out from the five wounds of the crucified angel. They struck the saint's side, as well as both of his hands and feet, which were forever marked with our Lord's stigmata.[187]

---

[186] Augustine, quoted in Thomas Aquinas, *Summa Theologica*, III, q. 54, art. 4.

[187] See Thomas of Celano, *The First Life of St. Francis* 2, 3, 94.

In April 1560, St. Teresa of Ávila experienced "transverbera-tion," i.e., the wound of Jesus' pierced Heart; she talked about this in her autobiography:

> I saw an angel close by me, on my left side, in bodily form.... He was not large, but small of stature, and most beautiful — his face burning, as if he were one of the high-est angels, who seem to be all of fire.... I saw in his hand a long spear of gold, and at the iron's point there seemed to be a little fire. He appeared to me to be thrusting it at times into my heart and to pierce my very entrails; when he drew it out, he seemed to draw them out also, and to leave me all on fire with a great love of God.[188]

In September 1918, Padre Pio received the vision of a seraph, who left a trace of the marks of Christ's Passion in his flesh (Padre Pio had already invisibly felt them). This time, blood flowed from his hands, feet, and side. This lasted fifty years. To hide his hands, he wore his famous brown woolen gloves. The stigmata are a special and rare honor. But we are all called to bear our own wounds as marks of glory and love:

> Perhaps in that kingdom we shall see on the bodies of the Martyrs the traces of the wounds which they bore for Christ's name: because it will not be a deformity, but a dignity in them; and a certain kind of beauty will shine in them, in the body, though not of the body.[189]

---

[188] Teresa of Ávila, *The Book of Her Life*, chap. 29.
[189] Augustine, quoted in Thomas Aquinas, *Summa Theologica*, III, q. 54, art. 4.

Suffering that is not offered and united to Jesus' suffering is sad, stressful, and lonely:

I see an enormous number of crucified people in the world. But I see few of them who are crucified for the love of Jesus.... Happy are those who live and die on a cross with Jesus. If you bear your cross with love, like Jesus, and embrace it and cherish it with all your heart, in honor of and in union with the same love with which He accepted and bore it for you, you will be among them.[190]

Marthe Robin, who received the stigmata in her thirties, recalled that it is not the Cross that we must love:

"Marthe," a visitor said to her, "help us to love the Cross."
"Oh no! We must love Jesus on the Cross! It is Jesus that we embrace and cherish with our whole heart."

Prayer

Dying of Love is a truly sweet martyrdom,
And that is the one I wish to suffer.
O Cherubim! Tune your lyre,
For I sense my exile is about to end! . . .
Flame of Love, consume me unceasingly.
Life of an instant, your burden is so heavy to me!
Divine Jesus, make my dream come true:
To die of Love![191]

---

[190] John Eudes, letter to Madame de Budon.
[191] St. Thérèse of the Child Jesus and the Holy Face, poem 17, "Vivre d'amour" [Living on love], stanza 14.

Selected Bibliography

"Les anges." *Dieu est Amour*, no. 14, 1979.

Aquinas, Thomas. *Summa Theologica*. Trans. Fathers of the English Dominican Province. 2nd rev. ed. 1920. New Advent. https://www.newadvent.org/summa/.

Bazin, Martine. *Saint Michel, protégez la France*. Paris: Éditions Pierre Téqui, 2017.

Bénéton, Marie-Sabine. *Les belles apparitions des anges*. Paris: Éditions Pierre Téqui, 2002.

Haumonté, Odile. *Nos saintes anges gardiens*. Paris: Éditions Pierre Téqui, 2019.

Huber, Georges. *Mon ange marchera devant toi*. Paris: Éditions Saint-Paul, 1969.

Lonsdale, Michael. *Sur les ailes de la beauté (Les anges dans l'art)*. Paris: Éditions Philippe Rey, 2018.

Mon ami secret—Une histoire d'ange gardien. NS Video.

De Muizon François. *Benoîte Rencurel. Une vie avec les anges*. Paris: Salvator, 2014.

Siena, Giovanni P. *Bonjour, Padre Pio!* Paris: Éd. du Vieux Colombier, 1960.

———. *Padre Pio, "Voici l'heure des anges."* Paris: Éditions Pierre Téqui, 2015.

Timbal, Nicole. *Les anges, messagers de lumière*. Paris: EdB, 2011.
Van Dijk, Hubert. *Mon ange gardien. Un ami, un guide*. Paris:
Éditions Pierre Téqui, 2015. Cartoon DVD:

About the Author

Odile Haumonté is the mother of five children. She works as a Catholic publisher and is the editor-in-chief of the magazine *Patapon*, which is designed to enable people to grow as a family with Jesus. She is the author of about fifty books, including biographies and novels.

Sophia Institute

Sophia Institute is a nonprofit institution that seeks to nurture the spiritual, moral, and cultural life of souls and to spread the gospel of Christ in conformity with the authentic teachings of the Roman Catholic Church.

Sophia Institute Press fulfills this mission by offering translations, reprints, and new publications that afford readers a rich source of the enduring wisdom of mankind.

Sophia Institute also operates the popular online resource CatholicExchange.com. *Catholic Exchange* provides world news from a Catholic perspective as well as daily devotionals and articles that will help readers to grow in holiness and live a life consistent with the teachings of the Church.

In 2013, Sophia Institute launched Sophia Institute for Teachers to renew and rebuild Catholic culture through service to Catholic education. With the goal of nurturing the spiritual, moral, and cultural life of souls, and an abiding respect for the role and work of teachers, we strive to provide materials and programs that are at once enlightening to the mind and ennobling to the heart; faithful and complete, as well as useful and practical.

Sophia Institute gratefully recognizes the Solidarity Association for preserving and encouraging the growth of our apostolate over the course of many years. Without their generous and timely support, this book would not be in your hands.

www.SophiaInstitute.com
www.CatholicExchange.com
www.SophiaInstituteforTeachers.org

Sophia Institute Press® is a registered trademark of Sophia Institute.
Sophia Institute is a tax-exempt institution as defined by the Internal Revenue Code, Section 501(c)(3). Tax ID 22-2548708.

SERAPHIM - pg 35